Life's Best Chapter

Retirement

JOHNNIE C. GODWIN

Life's Best Chapter

Retirement

JOHNNIE C. GODWIN

New Hope® Publishers
Birmingham, Alabama

New Hope® Publishers
P.O. Box 12065
Birmingham, AL 35202-2065
www.newhopepubl.com

Library of Congress Cataloging-in-Publication Data
Godwin, Johnnie C.
  Life's best chapter, retirement / Johnnie C. Godwin.
    p. cm.
  ISBN 1-56309-717-6
  1. Retirees--Religious life. 2. Retirement--Religious
aspects--Christianity. I. Title.
BV4596.R47 .G64 2000
248.8'5--dc21
                                    00-010550

Cover design by Teresa Brooks

ISBN: 1-56309-717-6
N004113•0900•10M1

To Phyllis,

My better two-thirds for
more than forty-four years
of marriage—and the one
I hope to continue loving
and living with in her
semi-retirement until
God makes it complete.

With all my love,
Johnnie
New Year's Day, 2000

Contents

Preface

When New Hope Publishers invited me to write a book on productive retirement, I was glad to accept the invitation. I felt that such a book could make a positive difference in one's retirement life and in the lives of those we share it with. Now that I've written this book, I can honestly say that it has already made a positive difference in my own retirement. *How so?* you may ask.

I began writing this book while in my seventh year of retirement. Looking back on the joys and struggles of those seven years, the folly and the fun, the productivity and the futility, I was able to write out of my own experiences and perspective. I also researched books, articles, Internet sites, and the lives of others to gain a broader insight and objectivity in discovering how to lead a productive life during one's retirement. This process has already helped Phyllis and me in our own efforts to live more productive lives as retired persons.

This book does not begin by talking about finances and how to make your money last as long as you do. Neither is it a list of 101 things to do in your retirement. Instead, this book focuses on our lifestyles, exploring ways we can balance our leisure and productivity in retirement as we respond to God's continuing call in our lives (see Ephesians 4:1).

Speaking of balance, let me offer a word of explanation concerning the nature of this book. I'm a retired husband who came home to join my homemaking wife, Phyllis. How can I provide a balanced and unbiased treatment of retirement for women from all walks of life? Some are homemakers, some are married, and some are single. Many are leaving a career or full- or part-time jobs. Some have never married but are retired survivors in their home, to mention just a few situations. Further, how can one retired male adequately speak to working couples who retire? There are two-income couples who retire at the same time, some who retire at different times, and a variety of other scenarios.

My answer is that I can't be totally unbiased, balanced, experienced, and knowledgeable in all these areas. But I speak from experience about my own retirement and that of my homemaking wife. I have interviewed others and reported their experiences. And I have tried to bring my research data together with the witnesses of everyday people.

Though I write as a male, I try not to be gender-biased in my conclusions. In a sense, Phyllis has been my coauthor, bringing her perspectives as a woman to this book. Still, I ask you to be charitable where I fail to meet your gender-specific or other needs in this book.

Now after seven years of retirement and a year spent writing this book, I've decided to take another sabbatical—in the sense that you will read about in Chapter One. Rest from retirement? Rest from productive retirement? Not really. Rather, I've decided to do something *different* in order to lead a more productive retirement (*Deo volente*). I'm renewing my weekly newspaper column on "Words and Things," doing some interim pastoring, joining Phyllis for more time on Godwin's Mountain and some day trips within our home state of Tennessee, and I hope to visit family and do more grandparenting. Thus, by "sabbatical" I mean doing something different to blend leisure, work, and new experiences in response to God's call in my life.

As my friend Elton Trueblood told me more than once, "Each chapter of life is good, and it is good to know in which chapter you are living. I'm living in life's last chapter, and it is best of all." I can say "amen" to this for my own life as I look back on each chapter and now continue to experience the best chapter of all: *Retirement*.

May you join the Author and Finisher of our faith to make your own retirement life's *best* chapter. And, whatever you do, *choose life* (Deut. 30:19).

Acknowledgments

A book I recently bought contains no acknowledgments and is dedicated "To No One." I've read acknowledgment pages that could have profited by this kind of brevity, and dedication pages that could have been a bit more creative.

I've dedicated this book to Phyllis because she deserves it most of all. Although there is a world of folks I could acknowledge, I've tried to select those who have contributed most directly to the writing of this book. I apologize to those I fail to name.

Leslie Caldwell, my editor, recognized the need for this book and brought the idea to me. I'm grateful for her insight into the need for such a book—at a time when her own parents were retiring. Further, I thank New Hope Publishers for agreeing with me that we presbyopic retirees need large-print type—as well as other special visual considerations to ease the reading. The entire New Hope team has been of super help in bringing this book to publication and making it accessible to the reader.

It is traditional for the author to take blame for errors and anything else readers might consider blameworthy in his or her book. I wish to follow in this tradition. So while I thank these others for their help in bringing this book to publication, I ask you to hold them blameless for how I've stated their views, misstated their views, obscured what they communicated clearly, or skewed the context thereof.

Those who've been especially helpful in sharing their own retirement experiences and thoughts with me truly are too numerous to mention. Many of them didn't even know they were contributing; and though their names are not here and they're protected by anonymity, they may recognize themselves—or someone else like them.

My wife, Phyllis, has been my other half and has given good representation to the distaff viewpoint of a retired couple. I owe my own mentor, James W. Clark, special thanks for his general tips about retirement and for his specific suggestions in the area of financial guidelines. Linda Sandlin has been a constant sounding board and source of input. Copper Daugherty helped make this book possible in more ways than I can say. I thank Oakley and Charlene Williams for reading my chapters about mates entering retirement and for giving me their feedback.

And if it hadn't been for Dad and Mother, I never would have been here to retire in the first place. Besides bringing me into this world and nurturing me into adulthood, they've shown me many valuable things through their thirteen years of retirement before Dad's death. Mother has continued, in her widowhood, to demonstrate what full retirement is. I'm grateful to my parents for what they've taught me about life, retirement life, and a whole lot of what is in this book.

Only a former editor and publisher like me could fully appreciate all that goes into the proposal, contracting, specifying, writing, designing, editing, verifying, proofing, wedding text and graphics, publishing, marketing, publicizing, and distribution of a book. Though the New Hope Publishers team are too many to identify each by name, my gratitude to each and every one is great. Thanks to all of you.

1
Take a Sabbatical

Days of respite are golden days.
—Robert South

Whatever else it may be, retirement is a respite from living life exactly as you have lived it through your earlier "chapters." Retirement is a new journey in the pilgrimage of life. Though countless others have traveled this way, this is a unique journey that you will have to experience for yourself.

Nevertheless, I've made some notes on this "map" from my own experiences and have entered some notes from others who have made the trip. I hope that you will find some good tips as you read it. How you make the trip is up to you. But when you come to the end of retirement, I hope you will be able to say that the last chapter was the best of all.

The Chapter of Life Titled "Retirement"

Regardless of what has brought you to the part of life titled "retirement," it's a good idea to take a sabbatical. The root meaning of *sabbatical* is to cease, desist, or rest. After lengthy, productive, and tiring periods of work, we all profit by a rest. And after a lifetime of labor, retirement offers the chance for a change of pace, location, and activity.

After a long life of work, one's retirement introduces sudden change. Depending on what has brought you to the momentous occasion of retirement, you may experience euphoria, grief, confusion, anxiety, or something else. Regardless of why you retired and what your feelings are, the time is yours. You can choose to do what you want to do. God, who rested after His creation, gave the sabbath for mankind to do likewise. And when Jesus was tired, even He paused to rest (John 4:6). Enjoy this moment of euphoria. Take time to deal with your griefs, your confusions, your freedom, and your need for rest. Take a sabbatical.

A Presidential Precedent

When President Jimmy Carter was just fifty-six years old, he was involuntarily retired from his position. He and his wife Rosalynn were embarrassed, broke, despairing, and felt that their productive lives were about over—even though they might live another twenty-five years or more. In his book *The Virtues of Aging*, President Carter writes, "For a while we just paused and contemplated our lives. To pass the time we laid down a floor in our attic, became reacquainted with our farmland, and jogged or took long bike rides through the countryside, stopping to visit at the homes of our friends of past years."

In this way the Carters began their retirement with a sabbatical. They didn't become sedentary couch potatoes, but they departed from all-consuming work and rested by doing something different. For them this was a productive time.

Personal Privilege

Both work and retirement started early for me. As a seven-year-old boy I sold newspapers on the streets of my West Texas hometown of Midland. I continued to work hard all of my life until 1992. Then overnight, at age 55, I was suddenly downsized. This happened much earlier than I had ever dreamed of retiring. But I am not alone. Between 1990 and 1997, 21 million others also lost their jobs to downsizing.

I was summoned to a "no-preparation-required" meeting toward the end of a workday. At this meeting, the corporate officer I answered to and the human resources director broke the news of the downsizing to me. No one had said anything about downsizing in our corporation, and I was a vice president in good standing. I was stunned as the officer commended me for my fine career and excellent work, then proceeded to explain the trustee board's mandate for new leadership in our corporation.

As I listened in silence, the numbness of my shock turned to feelings of anger, grief, disappointment, chagrin, acceptance, and relief. I told these two colleagues that I knew it had been hard for them to break the news to me. Further, I told them I knew it would be hard for them to give that same message to others of my peers. I then took over the meeting by concluding it with prayer for those two fellows. After the "amen" I looked them in the eye, shook their hands, and left; and we're still friends. Later I'll tell you more about how this event—which seemed to be a tragedy at the time—proved to be a blessing in disguise. For now I'll just share that I went back to my office and proceeded to pull myself together.

Then I went home. A lifetime rule at our house has been that we don't ever share bad news until after dinner. Phyllis and I ate dinner and exchanged a bit of general conversation about the day, just as we always had. After dinner I told her that I had news that would sound bad at the beginning but would be good in the end. I told her I needed to talk with her about my retirement. With shock on her face and anxiety in her heart, she asked, "When?" I said, "Now." Phyllis's eyes welled up with concern. Our feelings were similar to those of the Carters, millions of others, and perhaps yours in such a time of crisis.

Phyllis wanted to know what we would do. In so many words, I told her that I didn't know over the long haul, but that for the rest of that year we would take a sabbatical. And we did. Whether your retirement is voluntary, involuntary, full, or partial, I strongly recommend that you, too, take a sabbatical.

A Super Sabbatical

Before inflation could affect us or other things could bog us down, Phyllis and I took off for part of a year to do things we had only dreamed about up to that time. We found a good price, and with severance pay went on our first cruise. We hadn't been pampered like that since we were babies. The food was so rich and varied that Phyllis was embarrassed at midweek when I asked the waiter if I could just have a plain old cheeseburger. I could, and I did. It was a second honeymoon after more than thirty-five years of marriage. We began to get to know each other again.

That was the beginning of our sabbatical. We had saved some money and were travel-wise in getting bargain rates. But the point of a sabbatical is not how long it lasts, how far or frequently you travel, or how much money you spend. (See Chapter 14, "Outliving Your Money," for a discussion of this matter.) The point of a sabbatical is to rest and take a break from what you've been doing.

When we got back home and settled in, I began to join Phyllis for her daily three-mile walk in our subdivision. During these walks I discovered that a vacant, one-acre lot we passed several times each day was for sale. The lot was a swampy eyesore to the subdivision. The ground wouldn't percolate, therefore it couldn't pass county health requirements for building a house on it. But the faded For Sale sign had a phone number on it. I investigated the asking price, negotiated a purchase price that was relatively low, and bought the lot—much to Phyllis's chagrin.

Then I began to improve the lot by cutting down junk trees, mowing grass, and having a curtain drain installed. I formed a team of everyone I would need in order to improve and prepare the lot for house-building. After several months I won the approval and sold the lot for a tidy profit. Today there's a fine house with attractive landscaping where that old swamp once was. This may not sound like a sabbatical to you, but it was to me. It was a different kind of work, and thus a kind of rest from the corporate work I had been doing. Besides, the project kept me off the street and out of Phyllis's kitchen.

With the frequent-flyer miles I had saved, we took a trip to Aruba, where the trees are bent almost flat from the constant winds. We snorkeled and hiked and shopped. We drove around and looked at wild goats and wild tourists. And before the memories of that trip had time to grow dim, we discovered a $448 round-trip flight to Madrid, Spain.

I had always wanted to go to Spain. So we went. And besides doing the tourist bit for twelve days, we took missionaries out to eat wherever we visited as a means of encouraging them. Besides this I was able to confirm an old preacher story about an ancient aqueduct in Segovia that still operates today. The only threat to the aqueduct's existence had been a short time of retiring it for posterity rather than using it. But since disuse was destroying what time and usage had not hurt, the aqueduct was put back into usage. The story is true and contains a seed of truth about retirement itself.

In between trips I became proficient on an Internet travel bulletin board and learned more about the U.S. Virgin Island of St. John than most of its natives know. We flew to St. Thomas and took the ferry over to spend an isolated week on this island. We got a twenty-percent discount off our hotel rate with the senior citizen AARP card. Again we snorkeled in beautiful waters, shopped for souvenirs, and ate dinner with friends we had met only over the Internet bulletin board. We learned what it is like to live without a phone, a notebook computer, or a pager. We were incommunicado for the first time in all the years we could remember. No one knew us, and no one could reach us.

We enjoyed these sabbatical experiences of our first retirement year, and they helped prepare us for a productive retirement. However it's worth noting here that sabbaticals are supposed to be recurring experiences. Further, a sabbatical doesn't have to be long in duration, extensive in travel, or expensive in cost. It can be taken in your own backyard, so to speak.

Mini-Sabbaticals

Though it might sound as if we were rich during that first year of retirement, we weren't. We were fortunate to have had some extra income for a brief time. But it wasn't the money that made the sabbaticals; it was the doing-something-different, and the rest that this change provided. Since then we have saved money for a week or two of sabbaticals from time to time. We've joined a travel club through which we get special deals that come with getting old enough to retire. We've also traveled closer to home, enjoying car trips to visit friends and relatives and explore.

Regardless of one's finances, almost everyone can take a sabbatical of some kind and of some length. You don't even have to leave home. You can stay at home or nearby—you don't have to travel a long distance to experience a mini-sabbatical. Some people who retire are tired of traveling. Airports, planes, and other kinds of travel remind them of work. To these folks, spending time in the garden or flower bed might be a form of sabbatical—something different from career work. Hiking, playing tennis, and moseying around—these and many other activities are refreshing and don't cost much.

Mini-sabbaticals can be lots of fun. You can take day-trips to explore sights, and most of the time be back in your own bed with your own pillow by nighttime. Or you can put a couple of days together and explore your own region or state. We did this when we drove across the Cherohala Skyway from southeast Tennessee to North Carolina. We had only read about the Skyway in a magazine. On that trip, we spent a night in a quaint North Carolina town and then drove on to Blowing Rock, North Carolina. That's where Jan Karon, author of the *Mitford* series, lived as she wrote; and we wanted to see the cultural backdrop for her books.

Closer to home we have found sabbatical relaxation by working at something totally different from our former jobs. Our three sons and their families each gave us one hundred dollars on the occasion of our retirement to put toward building a toolshed on Godwin's Mountain. (Godwin's Mountain is fifty-six acres nearby that we bought a long time ago but hadn't been able to fully enjoy because of work and lack of time.) We felt a little guilty taking their hard-earned money, but it was a gift not to be refused.

I looked at display models of wooden sheds to be built

on-site and eventually decided on a two-story cabin. The shell of the cabin was 16 feet by 24 feet; and we built it on the very top of our mountain. This was the beginning of both rest and work away from civilization—no running water, no bathroom facilities, and no light except by lantern or generator. We worked like dogs to make this place a good get-away, but it was all pure fun. This is another experience of sabbatical rest: doing something different, something that departs from the normal routine.

As Daniel Considine writes in his book *Good Advice,* "Find out for yourself the form of rest that refreshes you best." And I would add, enjoy the blessed rest without guilt.

Sabbaticals Without Guilt

Gene Fowler has said, "It is no disgrace to rest a bit." Many enter retirement unaware that they have become workaholics. In fact it may take retirement for you to discover that you've let yourself become a workaholic. Psychologist Wayne Oates gave us the word "workaholic," but throughout history many others have described this addiction. Stephen MacKenna once said, "I find I haven't the art of rest." Ernest Hello wrote, "To work is simple enough; but to rest, there is the difficulty." And Benjamin Franklin said, "He that can take rest is greater than he that can take cities."

As far as taking a sabbatical without guilt goes, I agree with St. John Baptiste de la Salle: "God…authorizes us to take that rest and refreshment which are necessary to keeping up the strength of mind and body." Grenville Kleiser said, "Periods of wholesome laziness, after days of energetic effort, will wonderfully tone up the mind and body."

Sabbaticals Have Reasons

Leo Tolstoy wrote, "In the name of God, stop a moment, cease your work, look around you." Mortimer Adler said, "When I have nothing to do for an hour, and I don't want to do anything, I neither read nor watch television. I sit back in a chair and let my mind relax. I do what I call idling. It's as if the motorcar's running but you haven't got it in gear. You have to allow a certain amount of time in which you are doing nothing in order to have things occur to you, to let your mind think."

Henry Ford once hired an efficiency expert to analyze his company. The expert gave a positive report on almost everything he saw. However, he mentioned that he had noticed that one man, whose office was a short distance from Ford's, was always kicked back with his feet on the desk and doing nothing. Ford commented, "That man once had an idea that saved our company millions of dollars; and if I remember correctly, his feet were in the same position then."

Idleness may be only apparent and not real. The wheels of the mind can whir in silence and stillness under the guise of laziness. I can confirm that it is important to learn to say yes to times of productive *inactivity*.

On Godwin's Mountain we have a large cave we love to explore. There's no need to fear running into any animals after the first couple of rooms. They don't venture into the total darkness and stay there. We see a few bats that have their own radar and come outside toward nightfall. Then there are the albino salamanders. They have no color and seemingly no vision. You see, living in total darkness means living a life without color, vision, or light.

Some folks allow their years of retirement to become a colorless cave of darkness—lacking vision, insight, and perspective. They need a sabbatical. It can be a year, six months, a month, or even a week or two. A sabbatical helps us evaluate priorities, gain perspective, and decide how to live life—especially retirement life. In order to know how we want to live retirement life, we need to know the alternatives and be bold enough to choose what to leave the same and what to change. A sabbatical can help us to make good plans and decisions for our retirement years.

A sabbatical itself is medicine to the soul. Thomas Carlyle wrote, "Rest is a fine medicine." And Harold J. Reilly ventured to claim, "Rest has cured more people than all the medicine in the world." For these reasons and others I urge you to take a sabbatical when you retire and continue this practice throughout your retirement years.

Sabbaticals Are for a Season

Sabbaticals are not retirement. They are for a season. In the academic world, and later in the business world, sabbaticals were introduced as recurring leaves of absence. The purpose of sabbaticals was rest, renewal, travel, study, writing, training, service, and the acquisition of new skills. They were not intended to be unending periods of idleness. The value of a sabbatical doesn't depend on its length but on the extent to which you are able to rest from the work you've been doing and be recharged for a new kind of productivity.

Sabbaticals are always
from something, for something,
and *to something.*

◄ *Reflections*

- Take time to remember all the jobs and work you have ever done. Which were the best? Which were the worst? How so?

- What is the longest time you've voluntarily been away from work?

- Why did you retire? Was your retirement planned or unplanned? How do you feel about it?

- Recall your best vacations, holidays, and sabbaticals. How have you envisioned your retirement?

Projections ►

- Identify retirement plans you've already made. Spend some time evaluating whether they will be adequate for living life's next chapters, which could last twenty-five years or more.

- Seriously consider a planned sabbatical to rest from career work, to get the feel of almost one-hundred-percent optional time, and to entertain the retirement possibilities that naturally begin to pop into a retiree's mind while the motor idles.

- Keep a retirement diary or journal to record what you may not remember; to retain thoughts, ideas, and plans that may come to you; and to log what may well be a happy and productive retirement, as a retirement map for your children and grandchildren to read and evaluate.

Retirement Words from The Word

Jesus said to His disciples, "The Sabbath was made for man, not man for the Sabbath" (Mark 2:27).

The master replied, "Well done, good and faithful servant! You have been faithful with a few things; I will put you in charge of many things. Come and share your master's happiness!" (Matt. 25:21).

Jesus said, "Come to me, all you who are weary and burdened, and I will give you rest" (Matt. 11:28).

Prayer

Father, grant us a sabbatical
"...far from the madding crowd's
ignoble strife." Help us to
"rest...till the Master of all good
workmen shall put us to work anew."
We thank you for creating
labor and crowning it with rest.
Amen.

2

After the Euphoria Is Over

Absence of occupation is not rest;
a mind quite vacant is a mind distressed.
—William Cowper

Marriage and a honeymoon are times of euphoria. Getting a diploma or a degree brings euphoria. The anticipation of a vacation often brings about euphoria. But as wonderful as these experiences—and others like them—may be, the euphoria is only temporary. After these experiences we have to return to the humdrum of daily living. Most of our lives we spend somewhere between the valleys and the mountaintops. This is true also of retirement. Let's take a look at the rites of retirement and consider what we can do when the euphoria is over.

Rites of Retirement

The announcement of one's retirement usually results in a fairly predictable pattern of events. As one enters his final year of work, he becomes more aware that he is doing these jobs for the last time. The rituals of retirement begin to take place. A typical scenario might be something like this: A reception is given for the retiree, the retiree receives letters from colleagues and friends, the retiree is recognized for his accomplishments, and he receives a plaque to hang on the wall—plus maybe a bonus with the final paycheck. Then he undergoes an exit interview that explains post-employment benefits. He then turns in his keys and credit cards and takes his "stuff" home. There are some poignant moments and many nostalgic ones. Then it's party time.

Planned retirement almost inevitably has a quality of euphoria about it. Although an unplanned retirement may involve grief and compress these rites of retirement, there's still some exhilaration about retiring. There is a break with the past as the retiree enters uncharted waters. Even though the new adventure might be scary and bring on some anxiety, there is still an excitement that stirs the blood and causes the heart to beat a little faster. This feeling might be compared to getting out of school for summer vacation; but in this case, it is getting out of school for the rest of your life. What euphoria! What exhilaration!

When my dad retired, he didn't do anything for six months. Well, that's not exactly true. He stayed in bed and read and watched endless hours of TV. (The average older person now watches TV forty-three hours each week.) He did interrupt his rest to eat meals, drink coffee with friends at McDonald's, go to garage sales, and attend church. Most of our family members were greatly concerned that dad would wither away and die because of his inactivity. I wasn't really worried, though, because I knew he was just taking a sabbatical.

When Dad retired, he commented that he had worked hard all of his life and had done what others wanted him to do; now he was going to do what he wanted to do. And he did. But after six months it was almost like the moment when Forrest Gump decides to quit running. Dad quit doing nothing and started doing things again. He had been a truck driver, and he started driving the church bus on trips. He struck up a friendship with owners of a mattress company and found himself making short-haul deliveries for them. When legal blindness overtook him and he could no longer do those things, he learned something every day by listening to recorded books far into the night. He maintained a sense of humor that blessed the lives of others. In these ways, Dad had a meaningful retirement until the day he died at age seventy-eight.

If the retiree follows the typical pattern, there's at least some time for pure sabbatical pleasure upon retirement. After this period comes the settling down and finding out what retirement is all about. When the passage from work to retirement has been made and the honeymoon of sabbatical is over, the euphoria will also be over. What then? This is the retirement question.

Paradigms That Don't Pan Out

A paradigm (PAIR-uh-dime) is a pattern, a model, a template to go by. Each person's retirement may be as unique as his fingerprints. However, there are common approaches to retirement that we might call retirement "paradigms." And at the front end of retirement, it's worthwhile to know which paradigms to avoid and which factors to include in your own retirement paradigm.

A holiday every day?

One friend of mine retired with plans to play golf every day for the rest of his life. He did play golf almost every day for six months. Then the golf got to be more like going to work than going on vacation. He wasn't happy with his retirement dream. So after thinking things over and looking around for a while, he decided to go back to work. Not the suit-and-necktie corporate kind of job he had known. He became the engineer on an amusement park train and loved it. He wore bib overhauls, a red hand-kerchief around his neck, and an engineer's cap. He passed his days making kids and their parents happy. It made him happy too.

My friend Copper Daugherty put it this way after his first year of retirement: "Johnnie, this retirement business is not all it's cracked up to be. I used to look forward to weekends, holidays, and vacations. Now there's nothing to take a vacation from." God made us for alternate work and rest; and without some kind of productive work, rest leaves us restless. As George Bernard Shaw once wrote, "A perpetual holiday is a good working definition of hell."

Aimless diversions

Besides the misconception that retirement is a perennial holiday, another paradigm that doesn't pan out is the unplanned retirement of aimless diversions. Few people retire with plans to indulge in an entitled hedonism. Most of us just know that we don't want to punch a time clock or take orders anymore. We want to be free to do what *we* want to do, even if we don't know yet exactly what that is. As we search for meaning in retirement, some of us gravitate toward shopping malls, garage sales, or coffee-drinking gatherings. Others of us let time disappear while we try to decide what to do. You can usually spot aimless-diversion retirees. They tend to look bored, empty, guilty, lost, and uncertain of where they're going.

The balloon-mortgage approach

I didn't know what a balloon mortgage was until I bought some property and was offered this method of paying off the loan. I decided against it. In a nutshell, the balloon mortgage process allows a buyer to pay a relatively small sum at the front-end of a mortgage while enjoying the use of the purchase. But when the term of the mortgage is up, everything comes due at once in a balloon payment.

Many people look at life and retirement in a similar way. They sell their souls to the company store, lead a life of drudgery, and work just to make a living. But they dream of a balloon payment of joy at retirement and feel entitled to it. In other words, they put up with an unenjoyable life along the way in hopes that they'll receive their pot of gold at retirement.

At least two things are wrong with this paradigm. First, the person who does not learn how to enjoy life before retirement likely will not learn to enjoy life during retirement. Second, death, poor health, or some other circumstance may interrupt the big payoff. The best preparation for retirement and old age is to live all of life fully and to celebrate each day along the way. Even an early death can't take away the fullness of the life you've already lived.

The boredom/old-age paradigm

I've noticed that those who are bored seem more prepared to die early than those who are vibrant with life. They begin to talk about how old they are. They say things like, "This may be my last Christmas." I once heard a retiree say in a bored tone, "I guess I'm ready for Freddy." Another told me, "People don't realize how old I'm getting to be." Both of these people soon died. Marie Ray said, "No one grows old by living—only by losing interest in living."

Voltaire wrote, "Rest is a good thing, but boredom is its bother." Those who retire to do nothing may literally be *bored to death*. When they get bored and stay bored, nature seems to accommodate their readiness to die. But those who keep on seeking purpose and excitement in life tend to live longer. Further, they continue to grow and enjoy a better quality of life. Though they may be growing older, they never seem to grow *old*.

The Right Retirement Paradigm

There's nothing wrong with anticipating retirement and entering it with excitement, joy, and expectancy. Chances are, most retirees have emphasized work far more than rest up to this point in their lives. Now it's time to syncopate your life by reducing the work and increasing the leisure. It's all right to devote more time to family, travel, sports, hobbies, recreation, and personal interests. God gives us blessings to enjoy, and retirement is one of these blessings. Retirement gives us an opportunity to share these blessings with others.

Our retirement paradigms don't usually pan out when they consist primarily of self-indulgence or unproductive aimlessness. Such lifestyles are seldom if ever satisfying for very long. Helen Keller said, "Life is either a daring adventure or nothing. To keep our faces toward change and behave like free spirits in the presence of fate is strength undefeatable." A successful retirement paradigm involves making adventurous choices; being willing to face change; and, yes, even initiating it.

Retirement does not come in one-size-fits-all. However, there is a paradigm that models principles we should include in every plan. I'll get more into these principles in a later chapter. For now, it is enough to say that the right paradigm does not include laziness or self-indulgence. It does include shifting our emphasis to rest and changing our melody to one that still includes work, a melody of hope, and faith to dance to it. The right paradigm calls for learning what to do with our time.

Learning to Kill Time?

My retiree friend Jim once told me that his father had instilled within him at an early age a sense of the need to prepare financially for retirement. So he did. But no one ever told him of the great need to prepare for all the *time* he would have in retirement. A retiree has many transitions to make. Chances are he'll be able to navigate through most of these changes and receive help in doing so. Whether it's dealing with financial matters, insurance, health concerns, housing, transportation, or whatever, most retirees manage to work through these processes one way or the other. But *what to do with our time* in retirement is another matter.

In his book *Learn to Grow Old,* physician Paul Tournier observes, "What each of us needs is a reconversion from earning our living to cultural activity." Tournier is referring to our need to move from working for a living to building a retirement life filled with significance and meaning. He points out that many people seem to think that leisure means finding a way to kill time without getting bored. Instead, he writes, retirement's leisure ideally should be used for self-development, progress, contribution to the human race, and finding meaning in life that survives one's professional activity.

Tournier envisioned retirement as a time of growth and productivity—not as a time of having to hunt for something to fill one's time. Not a time when family and friends try to ease you into the mold they think you should occupy in retirement. Tournier adds that the problem for retirees is not filling up time; rather, it is filling time with that which is significant and meaningful to them.

Long ago I read the proverb, "You can't kill time without injuring eternity."

For me, the divine stewardship of life is at the heart of what to do with retirement time.

A Developmental Task

As in the first part of life, all of retirement is a developmental task that calls for making wise choices. While still at the front end of retirement, we are wise to make a conscious decision to live on the top side of life rather than underneath it. Sara Teasdale wrote, "I make the most of all that comes and the least of all that goes." Though we will inevitably decline and suffer losses during our retirement days, we can meet these losses with strength if we strive to make our gratitude greater than our grief. Sara chose to welcome and give thanks for her blessings rather than wallow in despair and regret.

We are faced with the task of choosing what our attitude and approach will be in retirement. We can decide ahead of time to give thanks for the light rather than curse the darkness. We can choose to experience enrichment and add to our lives as we learn to welcome change and opportunity.

We can learn how to make the most
of our time and the least of our losses.
After the euphoria at the beginning of
retirement is over, it's time to begin
writing life's next chapter.

◄ *Reflections*

- Take a personality inventory. Such a process may be helpful at any stage of life, but it offers special help to new retirees. Why? At retirement, you might possibly have as much as one-third of your life left to live. It's a good idea to know your options for what lies ahead.

- Recall your heritage: ancestors and immediate family, parents' retirement style, a thumbnail sketch of your life—where you've come from and where you are at this point in life.

- What did you once enjoy doing that you no longer do but would like to begin doing again?

- Recall what you've enjoyed doing most of your life and career that you want to continue doing. What do you want to quit doing?

- Consider who you are and who you've become. List your personal traits, preferences, attitudes, interests, abilities, skills, characteristics, experiences, assets, and liabilities.

Projections ➤

- What new thing do you want to start doing?

- What are you interested in doing but not equipped to do right now?

- How do you plan to mesh your retirement life with that of your mate—who may or may not yet be retired?

- Now that you probably won't be leaving home to go to work each day, how are you going to match who you are with what you have time to do?

- The Dead Sea is "dead" because it takes in and doesn't give out. What are some ways that you can continue to live through sharing yourself and what you have with others?

You don't have to make all of these decisions right now. But be warned: After the euphoria of retirement is over, time will begin to disappear while you try to decide what to do with it. In order to live a productive and enjoyable retirement, you need to consider the decisions, goals, and commitments that lie before you.

Because you are human, part of a community, and a citizen of a nation, there are still some things you'll have to do. Because you're human, there are some things you want to do. And because you were created in the image of God, there are some things you are called to do.

Retirement Words from The Word

"Then the man who had received the one talent came…[and] said,…'I was afraid and went out and hid your talent in the ground.'… His master replied, 'You wicked, lazy servant! …Take the talent from him and give it to the one who has the ten talents' " (Matt. 25:24–28).

"Trust in the LORD with all your heart; and lean not on your own understanding" (Prov. 3:5).

"How long will you lie there, you sluggard? When will you get up from your sleep?" (Prov. 6:9).

"Finally, brothers, whatever is true, whatever is noble, whatever is right, whatever is pure, whatever is lovely, whatever is admirable—if anything is excellent or praise-worthy—think about such things. Whatever you have learned or received or heard from me, or seen in me—put it into practice. And the God of peace will be with you" (Phil. 4:8–9).

"Give thanks in all circumstances, for this is God's will for you in Christ Jesus" (1 Thess. 5:18).

Prayer

Father, help me to remember
the past with joy, but help me not
to hold onto it. Help me to have
gratitude stronger than grief, and
forgiveness stronger than resentment.
Remind me that You are not finished
molding me into Your image. Help me
to balance rest, recreation, re-creation,
and work. May I remember that
Your will includes earthly rest, but not
retirement from Your will. Help me
to be a good steward of what You've
entrusted to me for Your glory.
With hope and faith I commit
my retirement life to You.
Amen.

3
Writing Life's Next Chapter

Just don't leave it unwritten.
–Chuck Morris

As I think back to my first year or two of retirement, I can see how God was working to guide me into a different but productive era of my life. Even while I was on sabbatical and thinking about what to do with my retirement, God was using past friendships and experiences as a bridge to the future. Although our retirement was uncharted territory, Phyllis and I weren't starting from square one.

Retirees have a foundation to build on regardless of how different their retirement life may be from their earlier years. And for Christians, the same One who has guided them through their earlier years is there to continue with His guidance. The pages of life's retirement chapters may be blank, but the research for further writing has largely been done. So it's time to begin again.

An Unwritten Chapter

During the weeks immediately following my involuntary retirement, my diary records that I was asking the Lord to show me what He would have me write in my life's next chapter. Meanwhile, Phyllis attended a missions conference during those few weeks. Our longtime friends Chuck and Erica Morris were among the missionaries attending the conference. Knowing that I was just beginning my retirement, Chuck asked Phyllis what I was planning to do next. She answered, "He's praying to know what to write in life's next chapter." Chuck nodded, then answered, "Tell him that I said, 'Just don't leave it unwritten.' " Chuck's message made an indelible impression on me. I realized the importance of planning, deciding, and getting on with the retirement chapter of my life.

A Text for the New Chapter

At about this time, my publisher friend Art Van Eck called to see how I was doing and to invite me to do some paid consulting for his organization. As we talked about retirement, time, and what to do in the future, I mentioned that in life's pilgrimage I had a Scripture passage for every major turning point. Art asked, "What Scripture passage do you have for right now?" I didn't have to pause to give my answer: "Live a life worthy of the calling you have received" (Eph. 4:1). In the Greek text it's easy to see that Paul is talking here about *God's* calling—our "vocation."

Retirement may mean the end of a job, but it's not the end of a Christian's vocation. I knew that though my *job* had changed, my *calling* hadn't. When I came to be retired, I told people I wasn't looking for a job but was fulfilling my calling.

Your Other Vocation

God's calling is not just something that preacher-types, missionaries, and denominational workers answer in their career and retirement. A sense of vocation is not just for men. God's call is for all Christians, regardless of gender, age, skills, or aptitudes. Paul wrote, "God...gave us the ministry of reconciliation" (2 Cor. 5:18). This is the thesis of Elton Trueblood's book, *Your Other Vocation.*

No matter what any of us does to make a living or serve in the home or elsewhere, our primary vocation is God's call to work with Him in the ministry of reconciliation. "We'll Work Till Jesus Comes" is not just a song for preachers. No Christian retiree has the option of abandoning God's call to His service or His church (which Christ loved and gave Himself for).

Our Christian calling must transcend all of life's circumstances, including retirement. Every chapter of life must begin with God rather than with self. This is especially true of the retirement chapter. Let's get to the heart of what productive retirement is all about.

Deo Volente

The Latin language may have reached West Texas while I was growing up there, but none of it seeped into my experience. However, as I left home for further schooling, I began to notice the words *Deo volente,* or the initials *D.V.,* in books that I was reading. After some time, I discovered that these Latin words or initials stand for "God willing." For hundreds of years, people with wisdom have used the words *Deo volente* to express the fact that their plans and their very lives are subject to God's will. Ever since I learned the meaning of these Latin words, I too have added the term to all of my goals and inserted it throughout my personal diary entries. This phrase is not a platitude; it is fundamental.

The Bible continually points to our need to consider God's will as the foundation for planning any chapter of life. In fact, there won't even be another chapter of life unless God wills it. James writes, "Now listen, you who say, 'Today or tomorrow we will go to this or that city, spend a year there, carry on business and make money.' Why, you do not even know what will happen tomorrow. What is your life? You are a mist that appears for a little while and then vanishes. Instead, you ought to say, 'If it is the Lord's will, we will live and do this or that' " (James 4:13–15).

The idea is not that we make our plans and then present them to God for His stamp of approval. Rather, our job is first to discover God's will for us and then to respond to His call. Jesus said, "Seek first [God's] kingdom and his righteousness; and all these things will be given to you as well" (Matt. 6:33). As you reflect on your hopes and plans for retirement, do you trust Jesus' words: "Whatever you ask for in prayer, believe that you have received it, and it will be yours" (Mark 11:24)?

Plan your retirement according to the blueprints of the One who has designed your life. He has some blessings for us that we will not receive unless we ask for them. When we go to the Author and Finisher of our faith for guidance, we will find what our hearts really desire. If we are to find our heart's true desire, we must search for it in light of God's plan for us. It's a mystery, but what God actually unfolds for us will always be better than our greatest dreams. This is true for all of life, but it has become more apparent to me through my own experience of retirement.

The Unfolding Drama

You don't really know what you will do in retirement until you retire. Even then, retirement tends to be an unfolding drama. A colleague of mine, Jim Fitch, retired with plans to play golf and write for the duration of his retirement years. The alternating writing and playing golf worked out pretty well for two or three years. Then Jim found he had written everything he had to write and was tired of playing golf with the same group every week. Phase

One of retirement had been a nice blend of work and play, but he no longer felt productive or challenged, and he wasn't enjoying retirement to the degree he had hoped. He then accepted a call to become the interim pastor of a church. This developed into the job of full-time pastor. Jim and his wife both found joy in this new challenge.

Actually it was an old challenge renewed. Before pursuing a career in denominational church work, Jim had been a pastor. Now he is a much wiser and more experienced pastor. His first retirement plan panned out all right for a while, but he needed a sabbatical from it. And his wife seems to be finding happiness, fulfillment, and serenity in her experience as a more mature and experienced pastor's wife.

Among my retirement friends the word "golf" and the name "Jim" seem to go together. Another friend, Jim Clark, had planned to play golf every day when he retired. Now, several years into retirement, he played golf only twice last year and twice this year. Heeding his dad's counsel, he has done well in preparing for retirement's financial needs. But he hadn't realized how much time he would have on his hands, and consequently wasn't prepared for this.

Recognizing this to be a problem, Jim has been working to become a good steward of his retirement time. In his decade of retirement, he has done some contractual work for a few years to take advantage of career skills that were sharply honed. He has also donated bookkeeping work and hands-on construction labor for Habitat for Humanity. He and his wife, Flo, now work together on Habitat projects. More recently Jim has received special-ized training to help people with their tax returns. He does seasonal work for a private firm and for the Internal Revenue Service to help average citizens who need help. Because of the earnings test of Social Security, Jim earns only a pittance for his labor; but he does it more as a ministry than for the money. Jim and Flo are moving forward, doing all these things plus the time they spend with their children, grandchildren, and Jim's elderly mother-in-law.

These are examples to illustrate the fact that retirement does not come in black and white. It can become as varied and multicolored as the first part of life—perhaps even more so. What people do with their lives until retirement varies greatly. None of us reaches retirement age without having had chosen experiences, unchosen experiences, ups and downs, goals reached and unreached, griefs and gladnesses, and serendipities. Up until our retirement, our lives are anything but black and white. So why should we expect our retirement to be black and white—cut and dried? Chances are every retiree will find this chapter of life to be an unfolding drama filled with serendipities.

In case you're not familiar with the word *serendipities,* *Serendip* is the ancient Arabian name for Sri Lanka. A fairy tale is told of King Fafer of Serendip, who sent his three prince sons out to broaden their education. The three princes were always searching for one thing but finding something else—a serendipity—that was better than what they had originally hoped to find. These accidental gifts do not come to the idle but to those who are actively pursuing goals that seem right for them. I've found God's serendipities in my life to be far better than my best-laid plans.

A Drama Folded Up

During the early years of our marriage Phyllis and I hoped to become career missionaries. After years of schooling and hard work to pay down our debts, we had finally jumped through all the formal hoops and were ready to be appointed as foreign missionaries to Asia. But because of some health problems and other factors that I don't understand to this day, we were never appointed as missionaries. We grieved that our unfolding drama seemed to fold before it ever had a chance to open. Had we misunderstood God's will? What did *Deo volente* mean in our situation?

With our first sense of calling and personal choice gone, we did the best we could with our second choices. With the healing of time and the arrival of other opportunities, we began to make other choices that seemed to be God's will for us. Over the next thirty years I pastored a church, wrote Bible-study curriculum materials, worked as an editor of curriculum materials, and occupied six different positions in a publishing house. While those career years were fulfilling, we never lost our commitment to missions.

As Phyllis and I dreamed and talked about our retirement, we envisioned that I might retire at sixty-two—not later than sixty-five—and that we would experience retirement together. Besides the usual plans to travel, write, and enjoy sports, hiking, and time with family, we both hoped we would be able to engage in volunteer mission work.

Then the retirement that still seemed distant at age fifty-five became a reality overnight. And though the fact of our early retirement seemed at first like a disaster, it was actually an open door to God's serendipities. Those serendipities have included our dreams, but they have been far richer than we ourselves could ever have planned.

With Chuck Morris's counsel—"Just don't leave it unwritten"—ringing within us, we didn't hesitate to take a sabbatical. We had worked hard, been productive, raised our boys, and were now at a crossroads. We paused from our work to rest and seek God's will for the next chapter of our lives. You've already read about our sabbatical. Now I'll tell you how our calling has continued to unfold.

Retirement Serendipities

Within the first year of our retirement, a struggling church asked me to be their interim pastor and help keep them afloat until they could call a real pastor. I agreed, and Phyllis and I found joy in returning to a small church with a big heart and big dreams. During that time a publisher asked me to do some contract-consulting related to a Bible translation. I also began to write a weekly column called "Words and Things" for our local newspaper. I would choose an English word to write about each week and then devote the "things" part of the column to sharing the gospel—minus the usual stained-glass language—as it can be applied to everyday, ordinary matters such as school, family life, and work.

As my second full year of retirement began, I received a call from the president of a Christian publishers association. He asked me to head up a publishers' exhibit and delegation to the International Book Fair in Beijing, China. He also asked me to contract to head up an effort to promote indigenous publishing abroad as a mission outreach of a Christian publishers' association. Phyllis would be my co-laborer in this effort.

This seemed to be the will of God, so we accepted the invitation. Can you imagine how we felt as we crossed the Pacific to be missionaries to Asia in a far wider role than we had dreamed of some thirty years ago? Can you imagine the feeling we had of being free to display open Bibles in Beijing, China—the capital of the largest Communist country left in the world today? We also partnered with and helped equip Hong Kong Christian publishers to prepare for the July 1, 1997, changeover to the People's Republic of China. In our work with the Hong Kong Christian publishers, Phyllis and I found a home and a family. After our contractual work was completed, we felt we had left our hearts in Hong Kong. We continue to counsel and encourage the Christian publishers there as they faithfully respond to God's will and seek to serve as good citizens.

Oh, you may ask about our first sense of calling, personal choice, and puzzlement over God's will. We had everything right except God's timetable. We weren't prepared for what He wanted us to do until almost thirty years later.

The indigenous Christian publishing outreach also led us to Europe for some partnership work there with others. We participated in and partially funded seminars to train leaders in new Christian publishing houses that had sprung up in countries where Communism had fallen. And once again we sensed our role as missionaries to help spread the gospel where Communism had failed. What serendipities we were enjoying!

Before our 1996 trip to the Beijing International Book Fair, a nearby church asked me to be their interim pastor. It was one of those situations that seemed to mesh God's will and our good feelings about going to the church. When we returned to the United States, we accepted this invitation and concluded our formal—but not our informal—work of promoting indigenous Christian publishing abroad.

The church, First Baptist, was set in a relatively small county-seat town. Its history was rich, and its heritage grand. But the church had had difficulty in matching pastoral candidates with its wants and needs. I didn't ask about their past but preached for fourteen months about the unity and harmony required to be the kind of church God wants us to be. Phyllis was my unpaid but effective minister of outreach. We loved going to the church on

Sundays and Wednesdays. Every Sunday morning I would get up to preach and say in all honesty, "I'd rather be here this morning than any other place in the world." The church wanted to call me to be their pastor, but I didn't feel this was God's will. And sure enough, God eventually led them to a young "Timothy" instead of an older "Paul." When the chairman of deacons announced the secret ballot vote, he said, "For the first time in my memory, we have voted unanimously to call the new pastor."

I enjoyed being pastor of a church during my early years, but being an interim pastor was like being a grandparent.

Soon after the interim pastorate ended, I received a call from officers in a publishing house to ask me if I could recommend someone for the position of director of a newly formed general trade division of their publishing house. I had spent most of my career in this kind of work and did have a few names to suggest. After a couple of months had gone by I got another call to say that for one reason or another those recommendations I had given hadn't worked out. Were there any others I could recommend? Time was critical because so many undertakings had been set in motion that called for experience and direction. When I couldn't think of any other names to recommend, I left a message that I might be able to serve as interim director for about three months. Their reply was almost immediate: such a working relationship was an answer to their prayers. For the next three months I used skills I hadn't applied since I'd retired. I was also able to mentor skilled professionals who were new to general trade publishing. Further, I was able to work with the CEO of the publishing house to interview a candidate for the position of director and stay for the time necessary to bridge the gap until he could come on board as full-time director.

These serendipities were grander than I could have imagined or dreamed. But now it was time for another sabbatical.

Another Mini-Sabbatical

After Phyllis had spent our first years of marriage as a preacher's wife, she found herself without a role other than that of being my wife. My changing roles caused me to move from full-time work to fuller-time work. But Phyllis felt the need to minister in ways other than taking care of our three sons and me. So she found—and continues to find—her own calling. She established a nursing home ministry in 1971 in which she still participates. She began to teach English as a Second Language (ESL) and has led for many years in an International Friends Ministry. In 1993 Phyllis went to Japan for two weeks as a part of a Sister City relationship with Tsuru in the Yamanashi Prefecture. She came back excited and bubbling over and told me she wanted to go back when I could go with her.

So we decided to take a mini-sabbatical by visiting her former students and their families in Japan. I made the travel plans, and Phyllis wrote to twenty-two of her former students, telling them that we would be in their area and would enjoy visiting with them. A woman named Yumiko Komiya was our contact person. She speaks excellent English and had only recently returned with her husband, Shinji, from living in our area, where he had worked for a few years. A few short weeks after the letters went out, Yumiko informed us that more families wanted us to stay with them than we had days in Japan. We were treated like royalty and accepted as family in Japanese homes for all of our nights there. We were able to attend an evangelical church, answer questions in the homes of our friends about what it means to be "born again," and model the

Christian life in a way that we hope will bear evangelistic results. What a serendipity to Phyllis's ministry! And, interestingly, all of this took place in Asia.

The Divine Paradigm

Besides working on books and other writing, I'm still writing the retirement chapter of my life. Since this chapter isn't finished, I don't know how it will turn out. I do know that the indispensable ingredient in a productive retirement for Phyllis and me is God's plan for us, and so we remember the words *Deo volente*. We can't see around the corner, but we're still following the blueprint. So far we haven't taken any wrong turns or ended up on any dead-end streets. We have confidence that God's paradigm is divine. So we continue to follow it. I recommend that you, also, look to God's divine paradigm for you as the foundation for writing your retirement chapter. This chapter is made up of mini-chapters. Although you can't see your way to the end of the book, you can begin now to write it on the basis of what you do know and can see.

As you discover God's calling, you will find that retirement is not a dead-end but an interlude. It is not a retreat or defeat—even if you retire against your own personal choice—but a rest that will prepare you for further meaningful and productive living.

**Retirement is a time to retool,
re-equip, reorganize, and refocus.**

It's a time to write life's next chapter.
Don't leave it unwritten!

◄ *Reflections*

- What are some first choices you weren't able to pursue?
- Try to identify a second choice that turned out better than your first one likely would have.
- Pause to reflect on the serendipities that dot your life up to this point.
- What are your retirement priorities? How do the words *Deo volente* figure into them?

Projections ►

- Consider the possibility of returning to at least one of your first choices.
- As you continue in your Christian calling, what are some options that might especially fit under the heading *Deo volente?*
- To begin writing life's retirement chapter, decide on at least one goal that requires plans, actions, and a completion date. Put your decision in writing and share it with at least one other person.

Retirement Words from The Word

"I press on toward the goal to win the prize for which God has called me heavenward in Christ Jesus" (Phil. 3:14).

"Do not conform any longer to the pattern of this world, but be transformed by the renewing of your mind. Then you will be able to test and approve what God's will is—his good, pleasing and perfect will" (Rom. 12:2).

"I urge you to live a life worthy of the calling you have received" (Eph. 4:1).

"If it is the Lord's will, we will live and do this or that" (James 4:15).

Prayer

Lord, You are the Author and Finisher of my faith, which is my life. As I write this retirement chapter, may I look to You for both its content and how best to go about writing it. I pray that You will grant me the desires of my heart. But if those desires are not within Your design, not my will but Thine be done. *Amen.*

4

Unmatched Mates?

*Marriage is that relation between man and woman
in which the independence is equal, the dependence mutual,
and the obligation reciprocal.*
—Louis K. Anspacher

Phyllis and I were never single adults. Both of us had to have our parents sign for us when we got our marriage license. They said we were too young—and we were. But after forty-four years of marriage, we are both glad that we married when we did and that we have shared these rich years together. No two years have been the same; and though we've always been mates, we've often been unmatched mates.

An Oxymoron?

By definition, a mate is a match. So this term "unmatched mates" seems to be an oxymoron—a contradiction in terms. Nevertheless, the term "unmatched mates" applies in some way or other to most marriages, especially when the mates retire. The radical changes introduced by retirement may require more adjustment than were necessary even in the first years of marriage. Marriage partners must re-match and mesh with each other if they are to make the most of their retirement years.

Although we live under the divine imperative of God's call, we live with and among human beings. If we're married, we live most closely with another who is one flesh with us, our other self, our counterpart, our help-mate. Retirement spells crisis for this relationship. Not disaster, but crisis—a time for judgment, decision making, and synchronization. Otherwise, disaster may occur and the marriage symphony may deteriorate into a relationship of discord, tension, and conflict.

Clichés, Commitments, and Plans

One humorous—albeit serious—retirement cliché goes like this: "I married him for better or worse but not for lunch." Another cliché says, "I've got twice as much husband on half as much money." Over the years I have presided over many weddings, and what I said during those ceremonies was perhaps the least important part of the event. These couples wanted to get over with the words and on with the marriage. And in fact, the content of their vows wasn't really as important as the fact of their commitment. But the changes brought on by retirement will truly challenge these vows, no matter how humorous the clichés above may seem.

The unwritten vows of marriage are challenged in new ways upon the occasion of retirement. The brief marriage ceremony barely outlines the commitments involved in marriage. The details and subpoints come to be tested through all the seasons of one's marriage. As Ruby Dee said, "One marries many times at many levels within a marriage." Mignon McLaughlin wrote, "A successful marriage requires falling in love many times, always with the same person." And Andre Maurois observed: "A successful marriage is an edifice that must be rebuilt every day." For marriage, retirement is a time of clarification, recommitment, and getting matched-up again.

Psychotherapist Betty Polston writes, "Everyone has a financial plan for retirement, and a health plan; no one bothers to make a relationship plan." While every person will have a unique retirement scenario—singles retire, husbands retire, two-income couples retire (though not necessarily at the same time); everyone needs a "relationship plan" for the retirement years.

Re-marrying for Lunch

When the retirement season of marriage arrives, it's a good time to "re-marry for lunch." I don't mean that the wife should fix lunch every day for the retired husband or vice versa. Rather, I use this expression to illustrate the unwritten and unspoken agreements and understandings that will need a little WD-40. The lubrication needed by couples during their retirement is good communication and happy understandings. Let's look at "lunch" as an illustration of the bigger picture.

When I was involuntarily retired, I suddenly found myself at home for lunch as well as for breakfast and dinner. I told Phyllis at the very beginning that I didn't want her to change any of her life patterns or routines just because I was retired. Specifically I said, "Don't worry about lunch for me." She took me at my word.

Still, Phyllis usually invites me to share a sandwich, salad, or soup with her at lunch when she's not away from home at that time. However, sometimes she communicates via a coded message that we both understand. She says, "I'm just going to eat some fruit for lunch." This is her way of saying, "You're on your own. I'm not going to fix lunch today." This is fine with me. Sometimes I eat crackers and cheese, other times I go out and get a burger. And I have even been known to eat some fruit for lunch.

The main thing is that we're learning how to negotiate and communicate through the changed patterns of our life that retirement has introduced.

Unmatched Communication

Unmatched communication can be a special problem in retirement. Sometimes reading between the lines is helpful. At other times, we may read what is not actually there between the lines, and come up with false assumptions and negative conclusions. We must learn to be charitable and to give the benefit of a doubt in all of our communications as retired mates.

It is crucial that we pay attention to the quality of our communication as we enter retirement and work to improve it in every way we can. The fact that a couple has been married "forever" may lead one or both of them to expect the other to fully understand a grunt, a look, or a context that is only implied. Lack of focus on what a mate is saying can automatically block communication. Interrupting a mate can dampen his or her desire to even try to communicate.

Then there are the simple mechanics of communication that tend to go downhill as we get older. I consider myself to be a pretty fair public speaker. But privately I've noticed that I often tend to mumble and turn my head aside when I say something to Phyllis. Or I may head out of the room and talk with a volume so low that Phyllis would have to be facing me and able to read lips to understand me. On the other hand, Phyllis doesn't hear as well as she used to. For example, one morning I awoke her by saying, "Good morning, Sugar Plum." She responded, "Did you say someone's on the phone?" These days we have a lot of this kind of conversation!

When we're at our best, we laugh and say, "We're a pair, aren't we?" This kind of humor helps us see ourselves as a team. But when I'm being difficult to live with or Phyllis's patience wears thin, it's not that easy. If our efforts at communication become too difficult, we may cease in our efforts and an unwelcome silence may take its place. Good communication is a definite "biggie" in retirement.

Occupying the Same Space

Disagreements, arguments, and moodiness are a normal part of most marriages. But these collisions tend to occur more frequently during retirement, when both mates occupy the same space all the time. Before retirement we may typically have shared the same space overnight and part of each day. But during the day we have gone our separate ways: one at home and one at the office, both away at work, or some other scenario.

Retirement brings mates together in the same space in a way that can be claustrophobic—no matter how big the house! This matter of space is not restricted just to the home, even though this is a big factor. There is another phenomenon, which may best be illustrated through the testimonies of some retirees.

Among our friends, one couple was just beginning their retirement. The wife queried folks on an Internet bulletin board about how to adjust to retirement with her husband. She wrote, "Well, the husband is retiring. I've been at home pretty much alone for years and years. I have my own life. What do we do? How do we face life together in this house twenty-four hours a day?" This woman friend felt she had lost her house when her husband retired. She felt a need to reestablish her territory in her own home—which was, of course, also her husband's home. Further, she had previously had her own car. She lost this source of freedom and space when she and her husband decided to downsize to one car. She felt she had lost her home, her car, her independence, and her space. Meanwhile her husband was experiencing his own sense of losses.

One man responded to this woman's questions with some lighthearted suggestions that pooh-poohed the radical effects of retirement on marriage. But several women homemakers and women who had worked outside of the home offered thoughtful replies. One woman wrote, "The shock of retirement will impact you both equally but in different ways. Your space has been invaded, but he's been kicked out of his!" Another woman shared how she and her husband were able to anticipate the tensions they would face because they were so different in nature and had many conflicting interests. In a partly humorous spirit they drew up a post-retirement contract of what they would expect from each other and agree to. The wife summarized it this way: "We kinda did this as a joke, but it forced us to look at our need to have our own space." She went on to tell how great their together-time and their apart-time is and how they're enjoying retirement.

In summary, all the suggestions this woman received shared three major points: (1) Don't get too grim about retirement and keep on loving each other. (2) Give each other time and space to be alone and apart. (3) Find out how you most enjoy being together and spend time doing those things.

An Unwanted Shadow

Part of the problem that relates to space is the feeling that everything is a duet now; there's no such thing as a solo part. There may not be a collision; rather, the mate who used to have a home-and-sashay routine by herself now has an unwanted shadow. One wife wrote that she couldn't even go into the kitchen without her mate following her. The kitchen was narrow, and the husband seemed to want to do his kitchen chores at exactly the same time she chose to do hers. Then when she wanted to shop or run an errand, the shadow was sure to want to go along too. Her mate matched her moves so closely that he was with her at every turn. He wanted to help even when she didn't want any help. This match was so close that it didn't fit. Instead of having a mate, she felt as if she had a conjoined twin. This wife needed to breathe on her own and have the solitude that makes the heart grow fonder and glad upon rejoining one's mate.

From the husband's perspective, he was just doing what he had planned to do in retirement: spend more time with his wife. Also, he wanted to be a help. This is why he offered so many "helpful" suggestions when she started to rearrange the furniture, put up a picture, or make other decisions that she had been free to make alone through all their married years. And the wife's well-meaning feedback to her new retiree husband tended to evoke hurt feelings or sad statements such as, "I can't do anything right anymore." Obviously here is a mismatch that calls for loving communication about how to get our retirement lives in sync.

Reversed Roles

One husband who retired early wrote (with a smiley face attached), "It took me six months to drive my wife out of the house. I criticized everything she was doing as I looked over her shoulder....Finally she took a full-time job and left me home to do my thing." This retired husband went on to describe that he took over most of the things his wife had been doing, and she found that she liked working outside the home. According to his report, he and his wife are enjoying both their time together and their time apart as much as ever. He counseled "If you don't allow each other some space, you can suffocate your relationship."

This husband had come straight out of the business world and appointed himself to be his wife's manager. His constant reviews of her performance were more than she could take. So she made a choice that has seemingly helped her, her husband, and their marriage. Herbert Samuel wrote, "It takes two to make a marriage a success and only one to make it a failure." No doubt, this statement is true; but it is equally true that one person in a marriage can take the lead in rescuing a sick marriage. And in retirement, this is especially true. It won't cure all the conflicts, but it can help us to manage them.

Dealing with Conflict

Jimmy Carter recounts, in his book *The Virtues of Aging*, how he and Rosalynn, upon their retirement in Plains, Georgia, began to deal with the almost inevitable conflicts that come when mates share so much time and space together. He shares that they eventually discovered a process that seems to suit both of them pretty well. Sometimes they just talk and iron out a disagreement. Other times they take a recess and give the argument a rest. When they cool off and discuss it again, they are more able to calmly and rationally resolve the matter. He points out that they both have come to realize that there are some points of disagreement that simply aren't going to be resolved; and they have learned that it is best to leave those issues alone. This pattern for dealing with conflict is worthy of consideration.

Phyllis and I have, for the most part, followed this pattern in dealing with our own disagreements. Let me add that the friendship factor is most important in resolving conflict. If we're feeling friendly toward each other, most anything we say sails on by smoothly. If we're not feeling friendly toward each other, nothing much gets by without some offense taken. We try to avoid letting the cause of our conflict overshadow our commitment to friendship. We've learned to drop seeds of thought that might or might not cause conflict, then leave them alone until they've had time to germinate and grow awhile.

Phyllis is better at this than I. Usually, when the seed is sown, time has passed, and the fruit begins to ripen, she knows when and how to move in for the harvest. This approach allows for a happy harvest that comes in a timely way—not too soon and not too late, but when we are both ready to work through our differences—when we are ripe for resolution. At other times we may recognize that our disagreement has to do with our mood, attitude, tiredness, or a time conflict. At such times we have learned to negotiate a later time to deal with the issue.

Whatever the cause of conflict, it's good to remember this bit of wisdom from Langdon Mitchell: "Marriage is three parts love and seven parts forgiveness."

Unmatched Memories

Especially in retirement, mates should learn not to remember anything with authority. Nothing conflicts like memories. Mates who want to get along with each other soon learn to check with each other before they are specific about dates, places, events, names, or anything else when speaking. When they are in the company of others, they pad their statements with, "What year was that, Dear?"

Or, at the beginning, the padding may go like this: John says, "I'll have to ask Mary to help me with the facts on this story." Though we may grow accustomed to interruptions and corrections, this doesn't mean we like or appreciate them.

A classic illustration of unmatched memories is given in the movie "Gigi" when Maurice Chevalier sings, "I Remember It Well." Everything he remembers "well" is wrong—at least as far as his mate is concerned!

What can it hurt if we should allow our mate to go right on with his or her story and miss half the details? We might even smile and nod with enjoyment as our mate tells the story. This could put an end to halting speech, nervous eyes, and tentative statements. Further, such self-imposed silence or active, positive body language can free us up to enjoy seeing our mate enjoy sharing stories, events, and memories. Of course if it's a matter of life and death or grave danger, then we may need to correct or question the facts.

Proving that your memory is correct and that your mate's memory is wrong is a lose-lose situation. I've kept a daily diary since I was seventeen years old. And it is true that the dimmest ink is stronger than the strongest memory. But whenever I pull out my diary to prove that I'm right about a particular memory, I've already lost, in that I've offended my Phyllis. And from time to time my diary proves that my memory was wrong; then I lose again. The compulsion to prove that I am right may grow strong in retirement. Arguments may occur over things small, medium, and large. In most cases, it's probably better not to worry about who's right. As Christina Rossetti says, "Better by far you should forget and smile, than that you should remember and be sad."

Matched Mates

Ideally, mates are matched in retirement by a voluntary, mutual submission that strengthens the foundation of their marriage. The Bible says, "Submit to one another out of reverence for Christ" (Eph. 5:21). Although the Bible states that the husband is to be the spiritual leader and head of the home, the focus is on a mutual love and respect in which the husband and wife put each other first. The Greek word here for "submit" is *hupotassomai*. This means, literally, to "place under." I once heard a scholar say that this word was used in ancient times to talk about placing a foundation under something. Our job as husband and wife in all of life, and especially in retirement, is to place a foundation under each other.

I agree with Pearl Buck, who said, "Nothing in life is as good as the marriage of true minds between man and woman. As good? It is life itself." Aeschylus said, "When a match has equal partners, then I fear not." And as Henry Ward Beecher observed, "Well-married, a person is winged; ill-matched, he is shackled."

As good stewards, our job is to return our mate to God in better shape than when we first married. So match up…and write this chapter with special care.

◄ Reflections

- When you first married, in what ways were you matched? In what ways were you unmatched?

- With your mate, select a key word to describe each decade of your marriage.

- Separately from your mate, identify in two columns in what ways you feel you and your mate are matched and unmatched now.

Projections ➤

- For both mates: Swap your matched-and-unmatched lists with your mate for study without comment.

- For both mates: Without agreeing or disagreeing on the items listed, choose one priority that each of you will agree to try to match the other's expectations in.

- Choose some special way you will try to place a retirement foundation under your mate. For example, an attitude, an act, a new habit, or showing renewed love and respect.

Retirement Words from The Word

"Each one of you also must love his wife as he loves himself, and the wife must respect her husband" (Eph. 5:33).

"Husbands, in the same way be considerate as you live with your wives, and treat them with respect as the weaker partner and as heirs with you of the gracious gift of life, so that nothing will hinder your prayers" (1 Peter 3:7).

"May you rejoice in the wife of your youth" (Prov. 5:18).

"A prudent wife is from the LORD" (Prov. 19:14).

Prayer

Father, I give thanks that You have yoked our lives together in marriage. Help us at this stage of life to be sensitive to the ways that we pull against each other. I pray that You will continue to match our lives in all the ways that will please You and will bless us and others.
Amen.

5

Why Retired Men Are Hard to Live With

Being a woman is a terribly difficult task,
since it consists principally in dealing with men.
—Joseph Conrad

In all the chapters of this book I have tried to address both genders. However, in this chapter and the next I will attempt to objectively look at some gender-specific traits with the intent of helping both husbands and wives in retirement. Wives will realize that this chapter is only a summary, and that this topic really calls for a book of its own. Husbands may feel that another chapter should be devoted to "Why Retired Women Are Hard to Live With." But I've chosen to write out of the experiences Phyllis and I have dealt with personally in my retirement and coming home.

Besides, although the context is gender-specific, much of this chapter will apply equally well to persons of either sex who retire and join their mate at home. The purpose of the chapter is to help mates better understand each other and have a happy retirement relationship.

The Question of Agenda

On my first full day of retirement Phyllis innocently asked, "What's on your agenda for the day?" For some reason this question raised my blood pressure. I replied tersely, "I don't *have* an agenda for the day." And what's more, I didn't want one. I'd had an agenda for almost every day of my adult life. To me, retirement meant *not having to have* an agenda.

Upon reflection I wondered—as did Phyllis—why her simple question had drawn such an emotional response from me. She explained that she had merely wanted to know whether she was included in my plans for the day and how she might prepare to adjust her own schedule to mesh with mine. Her question had been well intended. Perhaps I thought there was an ulterior motive to the question—prepping me for my first retirement honey-do list. Perhaps the question suggested pressure to meet someone else's standards; and, after having had to do this throughout my working life, this bothered me. Whatever the reason, Phyllis placed this agenda question in her "don't-ask" box.

Since then, through sharing with retiree friends and their spouses, I've learned that this "agenda question" is a standard one that spouses of recent retirees ask. I've also learned that these wives find themselves at a total loss to explain why their husbands blow up over such a simple question. Now that I've been retired several years, this question is no big deal. In fact I enjoy pulling out my to-do list and sharing it. But it has taken me some time to get to this point. That first post-retirement encounter was just a hint of the hard adjustments that Phyllis and I would face. It also signaled to Phyllis that this male retiree was going to be a challenge to live with.

Many retirement households are like a minefield. If the wife is aware of and sensitive to where the mines are, she can avoid them, deal with them, or work around them. In this chapter I hope to help retired couples identify these minefields, those sensitive points that arise with the onset of retirement. Of course newly retired husbands are not always hard to live with, but frequently they are. So let's take a look at where some of the mines are and why retired men are hard to live with.

Because They're Men

Basically, retired men are hard to live with because of who they are, how they feel, what they think, and how they behave. I'm not writing to defend retired men and what makes them hard to get along with but, rather, to offer some insight and a few suggestions that might help.

Retired men are hard to live with because they're men. No matter what you or I think about political correctness, inclusive language, or equality of the sexes, the fact remains that men and women are different. Our stereotypes of genders may not always be correct. But without being rigid or sexist, most of us recognize some gender differences besides the obvious physical characteristics.

For example, my sister Marylyn and I machine-gun emails back and forth daily. But occasionally Phyllis will email Marylyn. When that happened recently, Marylyn noted with delight how glad she was to get Phyllis's perspective. When I asked her the difference, Marylyn replied, "You tend to write in outline; Phyllis fills in the details." Just a few days after that, I happened upon a televised marriage-enrichment seminar in which the male leader said, "Women want all the details; men just give the summary facts." Now if the subject is sports or cars or computers, men may put in endless details; but on matters of the heart and caring, I suppose it's fair to say we men tend to speak in outline. This doesn't necessarily make retired men hard to live with, but it does reflect a different approach to communication.

From "Somebody" to "Has-been"

Ask a retired man who he is, and chances are he'll tell you who he has been. Usually, he begins by telling you about the work that has defined his life and given meaning to it—his former line of work and his position. He feels that there's nothing else to add to his resume, which has been growing through all the years of his life. When a man has a title and a job—no matter how impressive or mundane—he knows who he is and what he is supposed to do. But when he retires, he is likely to feel like a "has-been." Seven years after my own retirement, I met a jolly fellow who had been retired for twenty-two years. We got to talking about retirement. He told me that he takes aside those guys who are getting ready to retire and enlightens them about what they're getting ready to face. He tells them: "As you begin your first retirement, you'll find that you are the dumbest person on earth and you don't have any authority. You're on Momma's turf." And though he's retired two or three times, he still holds this viewpoint.

We're fond of saying that a person is who he *is,* not what he *does.* But the truth is, we often don't make this distinction. A man's identity is all too often tied up with his work. When he retires, he loses his sense of identity. The retiree has to struggle to know who he is in the present tense. He needs to know that he is a somebody, not a nobody. He won't find rest from this frustration until he discovers a new niche for his life. After the euphoria of retirement is over, the unoccupied man may well tend to grow restless, irritable, unhappy, depressed, and become hard to live with. Fortunately, this stage of retirement is a passage that soon passes—with patience, time, and the right kind of help from spouse, family, and friends.

Disdain for the Mundane

When men are good at their work, they're proud of it and their accomplishments. But when what they're good at ends with retirement, they often look at common tasks as beneath their dignity or not deserving of their time and attention. The let-down from career pride is a humbling experience and takes some getting used to. Part of the retirement transition involves moving from the "meaningful" to the "menial" tasks that a person had little or no time for during his busy career.

For example, I signed a contract to buy a million dollars worth of fine paper for Bible publishing a short time before my retirement. Boy, there was a zing to this negotiation and contract signing! And there were a lot of other zings to the work I did. But after retiring, when I went back to my former workplace for a brief visit, the veteran security guard unconsciously put into words what had happened to me. She was talking with a young maintenance man when I came to her desk. She happily interrupted her conversation to greet me. Then she introduced me to the young man, saying, "This is Johnnie Godwin. He used to be important." I didn't mind what she said, but it reminded me that the corporate zing was gone—I was a has-been there.

Further, after Phyllis and I returned from our retirement cruise, the grass needed mowing. As I sat on the riding mower, I felt like the "zing" had turned to "ping." The only joy I found in mowing grass was seeing how well I could take corners with the mower revved up to top speed. The garbage needed taking out, and I did it. When I was at the office, someone else had performed these tasks during the night; I was never bothered with them. In retirement I was moved from tackling contracts, strategies, goals, missions, visions, and budgets to mowing grass;

killing time; performing household chores; and attending weddings, funerals, and what I call "pink-tea" affairs. I felt a disdain for the mundane.

Typically it's at about this stage in retirement when unasked-for counsel comes from mates, family, friends, and others. As a friend of mine once told me, unasked-for counsel is usually perceived as criticism. And sure enough, when the retiree has time on his hands and others suggest ways for him to fill it up, he feels criticized for the way he is spending his time. Or he may simply feel pressure to conform to others' suggestions about ways to fill up time. The retiree doesn't want or need something to fill up his time; he needs something to fill up his sense of meaning in life. His need is not for "busyness" but for significance. He has lost his sense of significance and importance. He had a former life; now he needs to develop a new life. He needs what he himself considers significant activity.

The retiree no longer has a *have-to*. His *want-to* may be gone also. And he needs the motivation of a new *got-to*. Suggestions about doing volunteer work; being a greeter at a store; or helping out at the church, chamber of commerce, or hospital may not hold any appeal for him right now. He has to find and choose for himself activities that hold meaning for him. Otherwise he'll be an unhappy camper, and he'll make the other campers around him unhappy too. This agitation may just be the ferment necessary to produce a new wine in life. But, temporarily at least, it makes retired men hard to live with.

Men Treated As Boys

Whether a man was a crane operator or a CEO, he was entrusted with a job and held accountable for performing it well. Typically, the job required him to drive to work in traffic, be alert to schedules, interact with people of all sorts, make decisions, and use his head as a responsible person. Whether he was supervisor, supervisee, or both, he was treated as an adult.

Upon retirement men often get the feeling that they're being treated as children—men being treated as boys. They feel smothered with instructions, reminders, and cautions. A guy may have flown all over the world and routinely made his way in rental cars to strange places in large cities. Now he gets directions from his spouse on where to turn on the way to the same church they've gone to forever, how fast or slow to drive, when to buy gas, and what to watch out for. He feels like a teenager learning to drive and not having the license that permits him to drive without help.

Husbands find themselves getting counsel whenever they go out for something. One may hear, "You ought to take something to read so you'll have something to do while you wait." The husband who is going to be outside thirty seconds between his car and his inside destination may hear, "You had better wear a coat, or you'll catch your death of cold." He may feel that his middle name has become "Don't forget to." The counsel is well-meant and probably well-deserved, but it tends to stir the "momitis" in the best of sons and husbands.

Another "itis" is "correctionitis." I refer to the irritation of constant correction over nits. Whether it's a question of who did what when and where, or whether it's some other kind of fact or sequence of events, it's a good idea to let the nits go. Give them a rest. Overcome the urge and impulse to jump in with corrections. It will smooth relations like emotional graphite. Otherwise, this constant correcting can become cumulative—like a dripping faucet—and wear down the spirit and the relationship.

Easily Bothered

While speaking to a crowd at a bookstore, author Richard Carlson was asked to describe the average person in two words or less. Carlson thought for a minute, then replied, "Easily bothered." I agree. Upon reflection, I believe my tendency to be "easily bothered" is one of my greatest flaws. We retired men may be hard to live with for this reason as well.

My dad was a great guy. He took in stride most major trials and tribulations. However, in retirement he seemed to get especially irritated over little things. I remember my sister telling me that Dad called her one day, all bent out of shape. The problem? The delivery schedule for his mail had previously been in the mornings, but now the postal carrier was delivering in the afternoon. Dad was angry as a bear. Most of what Dad got was junk mail, but he wanted it delivered early—as it always had been.

I'm a chip off the old block. I find myself more easily bothered than I like to admit. If we run out of ketchup, mustard, or other condiments, I'm upset. If people don't drive down the highway to suit me, I'm bothered. If the green traffic light turns red just as I get to it, I'm frustrated. I don't mean to imply that I'm always in an angry mood— I'm not. But I do confess that I'm too easily bothered. And this makes me unpleasant to be around—at least part of the time. The same thing is likely true of you or your retired husband.

Getting Over Being Easily Bothered

As a rule men don't *want* to be hard to live with. They know when they're being donkeys, but this doesn't stop them from braying. And when men get through snorting, kicking and fussing, and being stubborn, they're sorry for their behavior—whether they admit it or not.

If a man has been hard to live with all of his married life, he's probably not going to improve much in retirement. As Marjorie Kinnan Rawlins wrote, "You can't change a man ... no-ways." Natalie Wood said, "The only time a woman really succeeds in changing a man is when he's a baby." On the other hand, if a man has been a decent sort, fairly compatible, and fun to be married to before retirement, these traits shouldn't disappear upon his retirement. There is hope for retired men who are hard to live with, so that they and their spouses can make adjustments that will enable them to enjoy their retired life together. How so? I'm not sure, but I think I've got a clue or two.

My sweet mother is not perfect; but she is a saint, and she knew how to deal with Dad when he was bothered. Somehow they were able to work out a system that seemed to work like magic oil on troubled waters when he got upset. They must have agreed on this thing privately because neither one of them ever told me about it. But I began to notice that whenever Dad was easily bothered Mother would say, "Now, stay sweet." Dad would then back off quietly—sometimes even with a smile. And the man who had been hard to live with suddenly softened and took on a kinder and gentler way about him.

I had never discussed this with anyone. But when I became aware of my own tendency to become easily bothered, I decided to talk about this with Phyllis. I told her what I had observed between Dad and Mother, and added, "When I get easily bothered or sour, tell me to stay sweet; and I'll try to happy up." Now this might sound like a gimmick to you, but I want you to know it's worked pretty well for us. I may even have mellowed a little bit.

However hard it is to put up with the old boy, stay with him. And if you're the old boy, give yourself a talking to and learn how to stay sweet. Be humble enough to get a little help from your mate. Then the strained, cracked, or broken relationship of marriage can mend instead of deteriorate. As Cervantes wrote, "The worst reconciliation is preferable to the best divorce."

It's Not about Sex

As any wife knows, her retired husband is around the house a lot more than he used to be. In fact, it probably seems like he's always present—except when she needs him. This retirement matter of husband and wife being together so much brings to mind what George Bernard Shaw once said, "Marriage is popular because it combines the maximum of temptation with the maximum of opportunity." Retirement puts that temptation and opportunity together all day every day. This may mean that the husband wants to do a whole lot more love-making than his wife wants to do—regardless of how loving she may be.

Wives need to know that it's not so much about sex as it is about manhood. A man's feelings of virility can turn to feelings of sterility overnight as he makes the transition from being a productive worker to being a retiree. And if there should be any emotional or physical hint of impotence, this anxiety is compounded. Contemporary humor has expressed it this way: "The difference between the first honeymoon and the retirement honeymoon is the difference between Niagra and Viagra." But it's not really a funny matter, and it may be one of the serious problems that makes a retired man hard to live with.

Jimmy Carter shares candidly in his book *The Virtues of Aging*, "Now, well past seventy, Rosalynn and I have learned to accommodate each other's desires more accurately and generously, and have never had a more complete and enjoyable relationship." Carter goes on to share an incident that illustrates that retired men need to know that they have not lost their appeal. While signing one of his books at an autograph session, an attractive woman in her thirties appeared. She brought a momentary hush to the crowd when she told President Carter that she remembered his *Playboy* interview. Carter's candid and honest response to a question during that interview had cost him fifteen points in the presidential polls and had nearly cost him the election. The young woman then drew the crowd's laughter and a beet-red face from Carter when she added, "If you still have lust in your heart, I'm available." Writing about this in his book, Carter confesses that even though he was in his mid-seventies, he enjoyed this encounter.

Now, don't get mad at President Carter all over again if you got mad the first time. Rather, catch my point. Loving, faithful husbands still love their wives and want to express that love sexually. But more than the sexual expression, they want and need to know that their manhood and masculine appeal are still intact. Chances are the wife who goes the second mile in the area of sexual relations with her retired husband will get more dividends than any stock ever paid. And in time this facet of retirement life may become more copacetic than it's ever been before.

Focus on Mortality

When a man retires, he experiences a renewed sense of his mortality. He has time and opportunity to dwell upon the fact that he is only human. He knows that he has fewer years to live than those already gone by. He'll be going to more funerals for friends of his own age. He'll begin to pay attention to pains that he didn't have time for or didn't notice when he was working every day. He may develop anxiety symptoms that cloud his daily sunshine with depression. Or, heaven forbid, he may become a hypochondriac who talks about all his aches and pains and goes to the doctor a lot.

Now there's no denying that the body wears out and expresses its condition through aches and pains. Arthritis comes to live with some of us. Others deal with very real problems of heart disease, cancer, or other diseases. I once read that after forty, life is just one maintenance problem after another. My corporation's former CEO, James L. Sullivan, would say, "After fifty you hurt somewhere all the time; it just moves around." Still, most of us Americans are living longer and healthier lives than ever before.

But our minds—especially our retirement minds—may be telling us something to the contrary. If we feel bad physically or emotionally, we tend to be hard to live with. To paraphrase a cliché, "When Papa doesn't feel good, no one feels good." Living with an emotionally crippled person is a hard way to go. It's important to have a healthy perspective on life and death, on pain and feeling good. The most productive retirees refuse to be enslaved to their feelings—whether they're emotional feelings or actual physical pain. They come to realize that there is a lot of living to be done between the retirement they welcomed and the death that they may dread. Retirees need to learn to celebrate the present and focus on the positives. In the meantime, a wife's patience and care can go a long way to help her mate who is hard to live with.

Suggestions

I don't have a pat solution or panacea to offer wives who face the hard task of living with retired men. However, I do have a few suggestions. These suggestions don't include any walking-on-eggshells approach. Living with retired men calls not for timidity but for loving confidence expressed in sensitivity and wisdom.

Keep a sense of humor.

A laugh is better than a frown any day. In fact, I counsel young people to look for a mate who wears a laugh more than a frown. This is one of the things that first attracted me to Phyllis, and it's still there.

Shake it off.

Everybody has problems, so don't be a wimp about it. The book of each person's life has good pages and bad pages, but some people choose to dwell on the bad ones. In fact, a wife who claims she can read her husband like a book may not be aware that she's bogged down on the bad pages instead of enjoying the whole book.

Give it some time.

Time doesn't heal everything, but marriage problems brought on by retirement often just need a little time. They may disappear or lighten up. The nature and intensity of the problem dictates whether to meet it head-on or to back off for a while and see how things go.

Memorize some appropriate quotes.

I love pithy quotations that contain humor, philosophy, wisdom, or even chagrin. The wisdom of others can help us gain perspective.

To show you what I'm talking about, I'll share a few quotes with you. Barbara Holland: "Men can't do anything alone." Kathleen Norris: "There are men I could spend eternity with. But not this life." When Hermione Gingold was asked if her husband was still living, she replied, "It's a matter of opinion." And, finally, Henry Kissinger's observation: "Nobody will ever win the battle of the sexes. There's just too much fraternizing with the enemy."

Pray about it.

The One who gave you your mate is also the One who can show you how to manage when he's hard to live with. In fact, as P. T. Forsyth once said, "God has some blessings for us we'll never receive unless we ask Him for them." Knowing how to deal with a retired husband who's hard to live with may be one of those blessings.

Retirement offers new territory for conflict between husbands and wives. When these collisions occur, we are challenged to turn "difficult to live with" into "a joy to live with." Successfully dealing with this challenge is worth the effort.

◄ *Reflections*

- What attracted you and led you to marry your mate?
- What have you enjoyed in your marriage up to retirement?
- Identify any major ongoing conflicts in your marriage.
- What have been the best problem-solving processes in your marriage?

Projections ➤

- Think positively: List why you still like and love your mate.
- Identify the "minefields" in your retirement life that you need to avoid or deal with.
- Plan to use your tried-and-proven problem-solving processes.
- Lovingly suggest a code term or phrase that will help you and your mate "stay sweet."
- Schedule regular events you can do together.
- Renew your marriage commitment to stay together despite the conflicts.

Retirement Words from The Word

"Be kind and compassionate to one another, forgiving each other, just as in Christ God forgave you" (Eph. 4:32).

"With all humility, gentleness, and patience, put up with one another in love" (Eph. 4:2, paraphrase mine).

"Have unity of spirit, sympathy, love for one another, a tender heart, and a humble mind" (1 Peter 3:8 NRSV).

"[Love] is not rude, doesn't insist on its own way, isn't easily bothered, and doesn't keep a record of wrongs" (1 Cor. 13:5, paraphrase mine).

Prayer

Father, thanks for giving me a mate. You know my faults and shortcomings better than I do, and yet You still love me and forgive me. You also know that in many ways my mate is especially hard for me to live with right now. So I pray that you'll fill me with love and help me to become as forgiving as You are. *Amen.*

6

When Women Retire

*Man's superiority will be shown, not in he fact that he has
enslaved his wife, but that he has made her free.*
–Eugene V. Debs

The quote above is not intended to be chauvinistic or
negative toward women. Rather, the sense of the quote
(from the book *Say It Again* compiled by Dorothy
Uris) seems to be this: A husband most nearly rises to
his potential in marriage when he helps his wife to be
free. Or to put it in my own terms, a husband does a
super thing when he helps his wife know and share the
freedom of retirement.

Although women who work outside the home retire
all the time, it grieves me that there is a sense in which
many women homemakers never get to retire. This
chapter speaks to this concern, and I hope it will make
a positive difference for husbands and wives who read
this book. Women deserve to retire, too. But let's start
by looking at the *status quo*.

Women Never Retire

It's almost a truism that women never retire. And it's
easy to see why this common statement appears to be
true—especially on the surface. When a husband
retires, he leaves his work behind him and appears to
be free as a bird. There's no work he has to do. No

responsibility he has to bear. And his retirement plans tend to look like a holiday every day. He has no boss, has no agenda, and luxuriates in his newfound freedom. He is the envy of his unretired wife. One cartoon shows a man asleep on the couch while his wife, busily at work, comments, "He's retired, and I'm still just tired."

Take a look at the wife and her situation when the husband retires. She has had her own space and place, her own work routine, and a sense of beginning and ending to her projects. Although she's always been subject to emergencies that rearrange her plans, she's usually been able to have her own agenda for the day and work through it with some sense of order and control. Now, with a retired husband at home, things are radically different.

You already know about "Unmatched Mates" and "Why Retired Men Are Hard to Live With." But chances are that neither the wife nor the husband fully understands the new role the wife finds herself in. She doesn't see that she has one bit less work to do than she had before her husband retired. In fact she's got *more* work to do. She's got a husband underfoot most of the time, and he's either in the way of her work or creating more work for her to do—or both. And when he's not in the way or creating more work, he may be introducing chaos into her orderly routine and causing her to feel that she has lost control of her own life.

With the impulsiveness of a teenager, the husband's plans may change every fifteen minutes; and he probably wants his wife to be available to fit into those plans. He wants her to go somewhere with him or do something with him. Or he may want to go somewhere or do something alone and hasn't told his mate that he doesn't want a date. On the other hand, when the wife starts to leave home with her to-do list for errand-running or for lunch with her friends, her husband may insist on tagging along—wanted or not. His shadow may become a cloud over his wife's existence. What retirement fun for the wife! Unretired, and already tired of her retired husband.

It doesn't have to be this way. But first let's look at what one psychologist has said about the wife's retirement. It's kind of sad, but this stage of life calls for some realism.

A Sad Retirement

Psychologist Paul Tournier wrote that a woman retires when her husband dies and she becomes a widow. How sad! But true in a sense. Once again the woman has control of her life. She can have her own agenda; plan her day; click off her to-do list without interruption; and have a sense of organization, routine, and closure to projects. She can come and go when she pleases without being shadowed. She has less washing to do and less food to prepare. She can move the furniture around to suit herself without anyone griping about the change. She can go to bed and sleep all night without anyone snoring or tossing and turning to disturb her. She's still got things to do, but mostly she has retired.

I've read enough Ann Landers and Dear Abby columns on this subject to get a sense of pre-widowhood and then how many widows feel about this kind of retirement once their husbands are gone. Typically the wives who still have their husbands write in with complaints. And before the ink is dry on the published complaints, widows are expressing how they now feel about the matter. Most of the widows would gladly exchange their retirement to welcome back a mate despite all of his faults. They would love to wash his clothes, cook his meals, feel the warmth of his presence, and even grin over the chagrin of his snoring.

They yearn for the love and companionship they no longer can have. With hindsight, they're able to see that retirement with their mate was a time of shared life on a different plane than they had known before. Retirement together offered a chance for the emphasis on work to shift to an enjoyment of leisure and optional activities for both of them. Of course in widowhood, what might have been and never was, now never can be.

So retirement by widowhood is not a happy choice for women. And though the absence of the departed mate may have made the heart grow fonder for him, there is no need to idealize the past or refrain from being honest about women and their own retirement roles.

Prepare for Widowhood Retirement

Almost half the wives in the United States become widows by age 65, and the percentage of women who are widows increases progressively in each generation (according to the U.S. Bureau of Census). There are more than 10 million widows in the U.S. and 175,000 new widows each year. Of course many husbands become widowers also, but the percentage is only about one-fourth the number of women widowed at age 65-plus. The reason for this fact is simply that the average woman lives an average of seven to eight years longer than her husband.

So wives need to prepare for the unchosen retirement of widowhood, and husbands need to help them. A good friend of mine works part-time for the IRS during tax season to help callers know how to prepare their tax returns. For him it's a ministry; and he offers kind, gentle help to everyone he can. In his work he has occasion to hear widows regretfully say, "If my husband were only alive, he would know what to do"—and other similar statements. When I asked my friend for his input, he told me to counsel husbands and wives to make plain and specific all the understandings and agreements they had had up to that point in their lives. Both mates should know their financial condition and all other legal matters that the surviving mate will need to know at widowhood. We'll talk more about this matter in a later chapter.

But without being morbid it's realistic to say that most wives will likely enter the sad retirement of widowhood one day. Most married women will experience the grief of entering widowhood. However, with good financial and legal knowledge and preparation, a widow will not have to experience other avoidable griefs. She will now be ready to deal with her financial condition, income matters, tax matters, property ownership, wills and trusts, and so forth.

While mates should fully enjoy their retirement together, they should also prepare for the eventuality of widowhood. But before the single status of retirement occurs, wives should be aware of the enriched possibilities for them in both semi-retirement and fully-shared retirement with their mates.

Semi-Retirement

A couple of our friends recently learned that the husband was being offered a special retirement package that will let him retire early. He decided to take it! Wife Charline was as excited as her husband about it. She shared the good news with me, and I gave my congratulations. She had also shared the news with her good friends at the beauty salon. She was both puzzled and dismayed at her friends' response. They unanimously bemoaned the husband's retirement by chorusing, "Oh, Charline, what are you going to do?"

Being a seasoned retiree myself, I can understand this concerned response from her friends. But I assured Charline that it was a good thing and that she and Oakley will have a great retirement time together. I know this because they already have a great time together. Further, I told her that it was her retirement too. She answered perkily, "Oh, I've been semi-retired for the last two or three years." She already knew the secret of a wife's retirement and had an insight about shared retirement with her husband. She had seen Oakley strained in the vast responsibilities of corporate life, the hassle of many miles of daily commuting, and long hours of work. She appreciated her husband's career, but she longed for him to get a new kind of life and share it with her.

But what does semi-retirement mean for women? Well, clearly it will mean different things to different women. But within the context I'm focusing on right now, semi-retirement is a call to compare and contrast early and middle married life with present married life. For women married and with children, it is literally true that their work is never done. Even if the wife and mother has worked outside the home during all her children's growing-up years, it would be futile to try to list all the other work she has felt responsible for and has done. She has been all things to all family members as she has tried to meet their needs and wants. She has been mate, parent, lover, friend, counselor, cook, washerwoman, housecleaner, emergency-service-worker, chauffeur, and anything else you care to add to the list.

As a rule, when the children get older and leave home, the wife is no longer all of those things. Despite the hanger-on children who live at home, the empty nest refeathered with returning children, and the possibility of caring for grandchildren, the wife normally graduates to a new level of existence and a better work status.

All you've just read may furrow the brow. It may not be true in your case, or it may seem just too abstract and different from your own experience. So let me put a little flesh and blood to it by referring to our own experience.

When I was barely nineteen and Phyllis was seventeen, we got married. Everyone warned us that we were too young to marry and that young marriages don't last, but it's hard to tell youth anything. So we went ahead and got married about forty-five years ago. We're still happily married and also retired; but, as you would know, it hasn't all been easy. For a number of years we struggled to make a subsistence level of living. I was still in school for the first eight years of our marriage, and Phyllis also went to school for two of those years. By our first anniversary we had just had our first son. And before I finally got out of graduate school, we had two more sons. Phyllis had to learn to be a wife, a mother, and sometimes work outside the home as well. But mostly she was up to her ears with work at home. I kept telling her that things would get better. And each time I said this she would reply, "In heaven."

Well in time things did get better, though neither one of us is in heaven yet. Through the middle years of our lives and marriage, the financial burdens eased. We began to share a few vacations, take some good trips, and get our kids to the point at which they could take care of a lot of their own needs. This was a different level of work for Phyllis, though still lots of work. When the boys graduated and got married, we found ourselves with an empty nest. And things got even better in some ways. We felt like we had gotten a tremendous pay raise because the food bill was so much lower. We no longer had to buy the boys' clothes.

And since we didn't even own goldfish, we could take trips together and begin to experience some of the honeymoon times that were supposed to be present at the beginning of marriage. Grandchildren came along, and that was enriching too. Things were better.

I got Phyllis a microwave oven. She began to use it regularly, and most of the time big meals were appropriately a thing of the past. We began to eat out more often, and that took some burden off the cooking and dish-washing.

While Phyllis certainly wasn't retired, you might say that she was semi-retired. She had plenty of volunteer work and stayed productively busy, but her activities were pretty much optional; and she had more leisure time for herself or to spend with me. Charline's married career was a good bit like Phyllis's married career, so I understood what she meant when she said she had been pretty much semi-retired the last two or three years. Even semi-retirement is not the shared, full retirement possible for loving, compatible mates.

Full Retirement

How can a woman ever fully retire? The answer to this question depends largely on what full retirement is. Every year millions of women retire from jobs outside the home, so they are fully retired from full-time, gainful employment. But any woman who is married or responsible for a household understands the nature of the question: Can a woman retire in leisure like her husband retires and not have to have an agenda? That's pretty much the question.

The answer to the question is no—unless a woman has a good understanding of what full retirement is. Further, the answer is still no unless she and her husband reach a happy agreement on a fully *shared* retirement. But with these caveats in mind, the answer can be yes: A woman can fully share retirement with her mate—and not just alone if she becomes a widow.

Retirement Caveats for Women

A caveat is a qualifier. The first qualifier I gave was that a woman has to have a good understanding of what full retirement is. So I would ask a woman to define what full retirement for her would mean. What would it include? What would it exclude? What would it mean for a woman to say she is fully retired?

I haven't taken a survey on this matter, but I am willing to guess that we might summarize full retirement for a woman: The wife wouldn't have to do anything that the husband didn't have to do. She wouldn't have to do anything for him that he didn't have to do for her. She would be able to do whatever she wanted to do, whenever she wanted to do it, and not have to answer to a boss—or a husband. Would this be full retirement for a woman?

To be more specific and practical, the wife wouldn't have to continue housework. No cooking, no washing dishes or clothes, no making up of beds, no vacuuming or dusting, no carrying out the trash, no mowing and trimming the grass, no grocery shopping, and no house maintenance. This doesn't cover everything, but it's a pretty good list. Full retirement?

Full-Retirement Misconceptions

Full retirement does not mean a holiday every day, no responsibilities, and complete rest. It may appear that way if the mate is selfish enough to take a sabbatical that doesn't equally include his wife. It may appear that way if the mate models a self-indulgent retirement. But that is not the kind of retirement you've read about in this book for either mate. Husbands and wives have a mutual responsibility to each other as long as they both live and are able to be up and about. Let's take another tack on understanding full retirement.

Expecting Too Much

If a woman thinks full retirement is retirement from all responsibilities, that's expecting too much and expecting the wrong thing. Neither the husband nor the wife is free to retire from all responsibilities or from reciprocal responsibilities to each other. But the reciprocal responsibilities do change in retirement.

I honestly doubt that any husband and wife will ever get to the point of 100 percent equality in full retirement. But I do believe there can be a *fully shared retirement* that both husband and wife can enter into as the retirement transition occurs.

Fully-Shared Retirement

It's not only appropriate for the wife to expect fully-shared retirement, but it's something she should say out loud. I would envision the wife saying with joy to her husband at his retirement, "I want us both to enjoy a fully-shared retirement." If that statement doesn't open the door to discuss the meaning of retirement for both husband and wife, it will at least plant the seed for cultivation. And when the thought is ripe, a couple will do well to envision the happiness potential for both of them in this era of life.

Before retirement the traditional role called for the husband to bring home the bacon and for the wife to cook it. Let this image stand for all the different things husbands and wives have done in pre-retirement as a general division of labor. With good financial planning and good fortune, the husband's days of bringing home the bacon may be mostly over; but the wife may feel she still has to cook the bacon. In other words, if the husband retires from work to play and the wife continues to have the same level of work, she doesn't have a retirement. Certainly not a retirement equal to the husband's. Something about this scenario needs to change.

Full retirement for the wife ideally allows her to share the retirement party with her husband. It's her retirement too. Without abruptness or abrasiveness, a gradual and mutual agreement on a new division of labor at home needs to occur. Full retirement for women exists only if it is a fully-shared retirement between husband and wife. What the husband was excused from doing all the years he was laboring, he is no longer excused from. It is not a marriage of mutual love and respect if the wife must continue to do everything she has done all through the marriage years while the husband does nothing. Even if the wife might be considered semi-retired compared to early and middle marriage, the retirement is still not fairly shared if the husband does not assume his share of the labor.

Men Helping Women Retire

I suppose Simone de Beauvoir was right when she wrote, "The most sympathetic of men never fully comprehend woman's concrete situation." Personally, I believe that a lot of men come to realize that their own retirement is incomplete as long as their wife, their other self, remains at work. As Elizabeth Cady Stanton said, "So long as women are slaves, men will be knaves."

Let me share a little personal history at this point. When I retired, I hadn't even been mowing the grass. After the boys grew up and left home, Phyllis took over that job. I traveled away from home about 120 workdays a year and was stretched from morning to night in corporate work.

Phyllis did pretty much everything at home, and I regarded her work as "woman's work."

After I had been retired for a while, it gradually occurred to me that I was doing neither man's work nor woman's work. I was just loafing while Phyllis was doing all the work. Being a decent sort of guy, I began to quit using gender terms to describe any kind of work. Work was work, and it needed to be done whether a woman or a man did it. My concern about my macho image went down the drain, and I wasn't afraid of looking like a hen-pecked husband either.

The grass needed mowing, and I knew how to mow grass; so I took over that job. When Phyllis sealed up a bag full of trash, I began to think I probably ought to take it outside to the trash container. Gradually I noticed that the bed was still unmade while Phyllis was fixing my breakfast. It dawned on me that the least I could do was make up the bed each day, so I took over that little job.

Now it's generally true—though there are exceptions— that men are not skilled in housework. Men don't know where dust resides. Their culinary skills are confined to digital cooking, which means dialing for pizza to be delivered. But in retirement, men who want to can learn some homemaking skills.

For example, as Phyllis continued her busy volunteer work outside the home, I began to think that perhaps I could learn to vacuum the floor. While Phyllis was gone, I began to experiment at vacuuming. Right up front I found that I didn't like the vacuum cleaner we had; it wasn't powerful enough. So I did a study and bought a new and better vacuum cleaner. Then I began to learn how to vacuum and to do an excellent job of it. And old dog may not be able to learn new tricks, but a willing husband can!

Phyllis nearly fell over when I took the initiative to vacuum. She thanked me profusely and told me what a good job I had done. Now, men, this is not the time to beam over your new skill or to make a big deal out of beginning to do what your wife has done for umpteen years. Rather, it's time to pooh-pooh what you've done as being very little and to express gratitude to your wife for having done that chore through all your marriage years. Without wanting men to have an ulterior motive, I just want you to know that learning to vacuum the floors may be the greatest aphrodisiac you'll discover on planet earth.

After the first sabbatical of retirement is over, it's a good idea to let a husband discover some of the things he might want to do around the house. It doesn't hurt to plant the seed and cultivate it, but the husband needs to develop the initiative. If the guy is a bum and always has been, he'll likely remain one. But if both husband and wife buy into the concept of a woman sharing fully in retirement, then the door is open for a new division of labor and a reciprocal approach to their joint responsibilities.

The Joy of Joint Retirement

Since I now have much more leisure time, I've tried to take part of the homework off Phyllis so she too can have more leisure time—more optional time. Without splitting up percentages in a contrived division of labor, we've moved forward happily to help each other. Now Johnnie Godwin hasn't arrived at Saint Husbandhood yet, and I probably never will. The point is that I've begun to assume a shared responsibility for the household. Some of the things Phyllis once had to do, she no longer has to. So she's retired from those activities. And although her retirement is not equal to mine, she's made headway; and so have I.

These steps toward joint retirement have brought Phyllis and me a mutual joy.

I will never be superior to Phyllis, but I have tried to set her free. This freedom is not the kind that separates us in any way; rather, it is the kind that is drawing us together even more. Every husband can try to free his wife in this way.

When Women and Men Retire

Besides all the work Phyllis does at home, she continues to teach English as a Second Language (ESL), lead a nursing home ministry, and lead in an International Friends ministry. Besides the work I do at home, I continue to do various kinds of work for pay and other kinds of ministry work for free.

People sometimes say that we're not really retired. In hearing this, we feel complimented; but we also hear the implication that they think of retirement as full leisure without work and commitments. Phyllis and I know that we really are retired. But retirement doesn't mean to us what it means to them.

It's worth repeating: Retirement is optional time to choose what, when, where, and how we work or play. The emphasis is on leisure time and how best to use it. We choose to make commitments and be productive with part of our leisure time and to rest, play, or travel with the other part of our leisure time. So we are retired—or at least semi-retired. And as we move on through the mini-chapters of "Life's Best Chapter: Retirement," we're enjoying giving mutual retirement our best shot.

Yes, women can retire—before
widowhood. And men can help them
retire. In fact, this mutual retirement
is the only way for "one flesh"
to experience full retirement.

◄ *Reflections*

- What was your thinking about women and retirement before you read this chapter? Any changes in your thinking? If so, what?
- Woman or man, what would you argue with in the chapter you've just read?
- Compare and contrast your workload during your early marriage and your workload now.
- Looking back, what would have been your ideal marriage division of labor?

Projections ►

- Envision your best picture of retirement for both you and your mate.
- Consider how this picture might change if you were widowed.

- Identify what you consider an ideal retirement division of labor for mates.
- Divide a retirement year into percentages of what you would most like to do.
- Complete this sentence: Women retire when …

Retirement Words from The Word

"Give her of the fruit of her hands; and let her own works praise her in the gates" (Prov. 31:31, KJV).

"Submit to one another out of reverence for Christ" (Eph. 5:22).

"Be ye kind one to another, tenderhearted, forgiving one another, even as God for Christ's sake hath forgiven you" (Eph. 4:32, KJV).

"Each one of you also must love his wife as he loves himself, and the wife must respect her husband" (Eph. 5:32).

"To every thing there is a season, and a time to every purpose under the heaven" (Eccl. 3:1, KJV).

"I know that there is nothing better for them than to be happy and enjoy themselves as long as they live; moreover, it is God's gift that all should eat and drink and take pleasure in all their toil" (Eccl. 3:12–13, NRSV).

Prayer

Father, help me to be more concerned about Your will for my life than about my gender. Help me to remember that I too was created in Your image and was created for rest as well as for work. Match me with my mate in retirement, and help us to love and respect each other in this special season of life.

Amen.

7

Body and ...

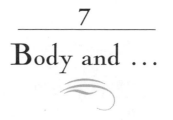

The human body is an instrument for
the production of the human soul.
—Alfred North Whitehead

Chapters 7 and 8 deal with having the right body-and-soul perspective in retirement. The focus is to keep your body in good condition during your retirement years. Although retirement normally includes living with a mate, a family, friends, or some kind of group, there are body-and-soul choices that no one but you can make. It's important to have the right commitment and make the right choices about both your body and your soul.

A Matter of Perspective

If a person holds a distorted view of retirement, he may consider himself old overnight and let his mind tell him what he can't do anymore. Philosopher Elton Trueblood used to counsel, "Don't retire from everything at once; rather, retire from one thing at a time, gradually and as you want to or have to." This counsel is especially important in dealing with the physical and the spiritual aspects of retirement.

Premature aging can come from disease, stress, genetics, inactivity, or a faulty retirement mindset. Inactivity and a faulty retirement mindset are factors that a retiree specifically can choose to avoid. We all have to get older, but we don't have to get old or give up on productive living.

When Is Old?

Jimmy Carter answered this question by saying that "old" is when we think we are. Baseball great Satchel Paige asked, "How old would you be if you didn't know how old you was?" Bernard Baruch said, "Old age is always fifteen years older than I am." When humorist James Thurber entered his sixties, he said, "If there were fifteen months in every year, I'd only be forty-eight. That's the trouble with us. We number everything."

These folks are saying that age is largely a matter of perspective. The birth certificate and calendar tell us how many years old we are chronologically, but they don't tell us how much life we've got in us or how many more years we'll live. We know some cars don't make it to one hundred thousand miles, while others make it to as many as five hundred thousand miles. Every now and then I see someone on the road in a Model T Ford. Now I admit that the car is old, but it's still running and has life in it.

How much life a person has within him is reflected more by his soul than by his body. The body may show all kinds of wear and tear while the inner being might be better tuned than it was at the beginning. Without making light of the burdens of an aging body, there is a retirement lesson for us here.

Don't Let Retirement Cripple You

I used to enjoy reading the cartoon strip "Andy Capp" before our paper quit including it. In essence the cartoon strip was a satire about Andy, an unemployed worthless skunk of a husband, contrasted with the virtues of his hardworking wife, Flo. On one occasion, Flo is worn to a nub while Andy is going out to play soccer. She comments, "You always said we would grow old together." Andy replies, "Yes, but you went off and left me, didn't you!"

Husbands and wives can help each other avoid developing an old-age mindset. One lighthearted example from our own home came when Phyllis began to have difficulty reading letters on a page right in front of her. She went to see Dr. Burkett Nelson, our optometrist. When she got home, she announced somewhat gravely that she had "presbyopia." She wanted my sympathy. But I was already familiar with this word we get from Greek, so I knew this just meant she had "elder eyes"—eyes that are less flexible, which calls for bifocals. Phyllis's *eyes* may have gotten older, but she is just as young and mischievous as ever.

The husband of an acquaintance of mine had heart surgery a second time. When the doctor came out of the operating room, he told the apprehensive wife that her husband had come through the surgery well. Fearing that he might be a cardiac cripple, she anxiously asked, "Will he have a good quality of life?" The surgeon replied, "I don't know. I fixed his heart; the quality of life is up to him." The last time I checked, this husband was still choosing to have a great quality of life.

A Healthy Recklessness

Get an annual physical.

Many people have gotten annual work physicals and need to keep these up even if they no longer work for a company that will pay for them. Others who have worked inside or outside the home may have not had annual physicals. They need to get one each year in retirement. Persius said, "Meet the disease at its first stage." Proverbial wisdom counsels that a stitch in time saves nine, and an ounce of prevention is worth a pound of cure. Having said this, it's wise not to become obsessed about what may be wrong with one's body.

Don't become a hypochondriac.

The only thing some people seem to have on their minds is what's wrong with them. They're hypochondriacs. A cure I once read for hypochondriacs was to have a healthy recklessness about their physical condition. The point of this counsel is that people can make their minds sick by worrying about their bodies.

When the doctor diagnoses a problem, it's usually a good idea to accept this diagnosis and also the treatment prescribed for the condition. If the doctor doesn't find anything wrong, it's usually a good idea not to let the mind find anything wrong. Otherwise it's like putting the brakes on quality living while retirement life slides downhill.

Josh Billings said, "There are lots of people in this world who spend so much time watching their health that they haven't the time to enjoy it." Laurence Sterne wrote, "People who are always taking care of their health are like misers who are hoarding up a treasure which they have never spirit enough to enjoy." These quotes remind me of something that happened while I was waiting in a health-fair line a few years ago. An elderly friend of mine in front of me had just gotten the results of his total blood cholesterol count. He complained, "I haven't had a sausage biscuit in six months, and my cholesterol isn't down a single point." I said, "John, I believe I'd chance one."

My suggestion wasn't dietary advice but a plea for some balance between body and soul. William Butler Yeats wrote, "An aged man is but a paltry thing/A tattered coat upon a stick, unless/Soul clap its hands and sing, and louder sing/For every tatter in its mortal dress." There's got to be a time to clap and sing, or else what's the use of living? Meanwhile, it's a good idea to choose your doctor carefully and let him partner with you in *how* you clap and sing.

Choosing a Retirement Doctor

Changing doctors?

You may have a fine doctor and be able to keep that doctor right on into retirement. However, many people have to change doctors because they change locations when they retire. Others have to change doctors because of insurance coverage. And some people have to choose another doctor because they either outlive their doctor or find the doctor joining them in retirement. Retirees especially need a doctor they trust, can understand, and are willing to partner with in taking care of body and soul. Although no doctor will likely meet all your needs, it's a good idea to have in mind the qualities you want in the doctor you choose.

Choose one with a memory.

Choose a doctor whose memory is better than yours. Choose one who takes good notes and reads his file before he meets with you each time. Several years ago I had a doctor who took me off the blood pressure medicine he had prescribed.

At each of the next three meetings we had, he began by asking, "Are you still taking your blood pressure medicine?" I tactfully reminded him each time that he had taken me off that medicine but that I would be glad to start taking it again if he felt I needed it. Now, do you want to put your life in the hands of a doctor like that? I didn't, so I changed doctors.

Choose a model.

Our priority is to have a doctor with topnotch medical skills, but we should consider other factors as well. A doctor ought to model what he expects you to follow. The ancient Greek medical expert Galen wrote, "That physician will hardly be thought very careful of the health of others who neglects his own." Consider whether the doctor himself is fat, smokes, drinks, has a religious faith, has a sense of humor, is punctual or apologetic, and knows how to talk heart-to-heart as well as face-to-face. In short, choose a doctor you like, trust, and will obey. Choose a doctor who can detect whether you've come to him with a life-threatening runny nose or are really sick.

Choose a human being.

When I confessed to one doctor that I had eaten a cheeseburger, he didn't chide me but said, "Well, all of us are going to die of something, and it's good to get some enjoyment out of life." I liked that. But concern for patient health causes some doctors to be very strict in what they prescribe. This fact led Sir Francis Bacon to write, "The remedy is worse than the disease."

G. K. Chesterton struck a blow for humanity when he wrote, "Man does not live by soap alone; and hygiene, or even health, is not much good unless you can take a healthy view of it—or, better still, feel a healthy indifference to it." You and your doctor should ideally have a happy partnership.

Partnering with Your Doctor

Prepare for your visits.

Once you've chosen a doctor, partner with that doctor rather than let him be the boss and you the employee. For example, I prepare a single-sheet, typed summary to hand to my doctor each time we meet. The sheet is dated, has the doctor's name, my name, the medications I'm taking, any changes since the last visit, and why I'm visiting this time. I keep a copy in my files and give the doctor one for his files. And I tell the doctor what I expect, hope, or need to know at this visit. Your doctor will appreciate this kind of partnering.

Be honest.

You'll get your best help if you're honest with your doctor. The doctor needs to know all the prescribed medications, unprescribed medications, vitamins, herbs, and other remedies you take. The doctor can't help you if you beat around the bush about sexual dysfunction, male or female problems, or symptoms you had rather ignore than reveal. Be honest, be candid, and identify your priority health concerns.

Don't overexpect.

Although it's not too much to expect your doctor to believe in miracles, it is too much to expect the doctor to perform them. You and your doctor should have a pretty clear understanding of what you both expect. A woman in her eighties complained to her doctor about her aches and pains. He listened sympathetically, then responded, "You must understand, my dear, I'm a doctor, not a magician. I cannot make you any younger." "Younger?" she replied, "No, I'm asking you to make me older, Doctor."

Be resilient.

As you age, the doctor's report will not always be good; and chances are you'll have to learn to live with some chronic health problems. I once read that the way to live to a ripe old age is to get a chronic disease and nurture it.

Besides, some of history's greatest works have come from people who were in the midst of chronic, acute, or terminal illnesses. They would not let their soul be defeated by their body, so they won with their spirit.

We do not choose our diseases or traumas, but we can choose to be winners instead of merely survivors. We can choose to bounce back or even crawl back from trauma and adversity. We can persevere, have hope, and live a quality life despite having a body that has seen its better days.

Have an agreement.

When the doctor has done all he can and your body and soul have done all they can, what's next? Living wills can spell out the next step, but the living person and the attending doctor need to have already reached a specific agreement of heart and mind. The choice is yours, but be aware that "body and mind, like man and wife, do not always agree to die together." Personally, I concur with what Lord Thomas Horder said the year before I was born: "It is the duty of a doctor to prolong life. It is not his duty to prolong the act of dying."

The Best Rx I Ever Had

Thirty-six years ago a Christian doctor named Robert Bone gave me the best prescription I ever had. I was a seminary student who acted as if I were Superman and didn't have a breaking point. But I learned differently. A full school load, commuting 225 miles round-trip every day, supporting a wife and three children, pastoring a full-time church, and staying up all night caught up with me and led me to a doctor. Up to that time I didn't have a doctor because I hadn't needed one.

Dr. Bone said, "Johnnie, you don't have a faith problem; you have a physical problem." He explained that I was suffering from exhaustion, being overweight, and not getting any exercise. I told him that I didn't have time or money to play the golf he suggested. Then he said, "When you leave this office, drive straight to the nearest sporting goods store and buy a good jump rope. Then you jump that rope every day." Despite having very little money, I did what the doctor said and bought a three-dollar jump rope. And I began to jump it one thousand times every day.

Through the thirty-seven years since then, I have continued to take this daily jump-rope prescription. I've jumped the rope, shaking homes and hotel rooms all over the United States and in numerous foreign countries. Even today, when colleagues and friends from the past see me, one of the first questions they ask is, "Johnnie, are you still jumping your rope?" And I'm glad I can answer, "Yes!"

Our second son, Larry, said about twenty-five years ago, "Dad, one of these days you're going to get too old to jump that rope." I replied, "Yep, but until then I'm going to keep on jumping." Just four or five years ago Larry wrote a Father's Day article about me in which he says, "Not even jump-rope manufacturers can predict the performance of a new type of jump rope the way he can." And I'm still at it today—after wearing out a bunch of jump ropes.

What are the benefits of jumping a rope? I've lost weight, become aerobically fit, improved my hand-eye coordination, and started a systematic exercise program. The program is portable, is inexpensive, and doesn't depend on the weather. But a jump rope program is not for everyone. Through the years my testimony about this prescription has motivated a lot of other people to start jumping rope. Some of them have reported back to me about pulled muscles, sore knees, splinters, and other injuries. So I know that jumping rope may not be for you.

In my first year of retirement I read that older people often keep up their aerobic capacity but lose a lot of their upper-body strength. So I began to lift pairs of five-, ten-, and fifteen-pound weights each morning to maintain my upper body strength. Besides jump-roping and weight lifting, my exercise program includes doing floor exercises, playing racquetball, cutting and splitting firewood, hiking, and walking with Phyllis.

All of that is nothing to brag about, but it is my effort to maintain and develop the potential of my God-given body. For a productive retirement I recommend that you work with a doctor to get the best exercise prescription possible for your own personal needs.

Exercise the Body

Retirement Transitions

Retirement tends to upset our activity patterns and eating patterns. The body that had to get up every morning no longer has to. The calories expended in preparing for work, going to work, working, and possibly exercising at some health facilities during the day are no longer part of the routine. The refrigerator is now just a few steps away instead of miles away. I've observed that people tend to gain weight when they retire unless they consciously try to maintain or improve their physical condition.

Stewards of the Body

Some people love to say that when they think of exercise, they lie down until the thought passes. Others humorously say that they get their exercise being pallbearers at the funerals of their friends who exercised. But those who have studied the matter know that exercise can be a powerful factor in both quality and length of life. Although the apostle Paul didn't put physical exercise on a par with spiritual exercise, he did recognize its value (1 Tim. 4:8). Besides all that, we're accountable for the use or disuse of our bodies. The Bible tells us that our bodies are temples of the Holy Spirit (1 Cor. 6:19–20).

Philosopher Herbert Spencer wrote, "The preservation of health is a duty." Taking care of the body is a sacred duty that calls for self-discipline. Dramatist Henrik Ibsen voiced his opinion about those who neglect this duty: "People who don't know how to keep themselves healthy ought to have the decency to get themselves buried, and not waste time about it." Although my feelings are not this abrasive, I do strongly believe that each of us is responsible to learn how to take care of body and soul and then have the self-discipline to do it.

Keeping the Body Fit

About twenty-five years ago, my Phyllis began to be bothered with a chronic condition of poor circulation and limbs going to sleep both daytime and nighttime. I told her she needed to do some exercise. She told me she did housework, gardening, and other things that were exercise. But practicing medicine without a license again, I told her this wasn't good enough and that she needed an aerobic exercise. She took my suggestion and started jogging. In just a month or two the circulation problem cleared up. Now, a generation later, she walks briskly three miles a day and still has good circulation.

Some people think they're too old to start exercising. They have adopted a crippling old-age mindset, rather than following the good example of other older citizens. My mother started exercising twice a day when she reached eighty. She does stretching exercises fifteen minutes in the morning and fifteen minutes in the evening. She says it has helped her arthritis and relieved other pains. At eighty-five, she moves well and quickly. She still uses her favorite tool, a grubbing hoe, and does a lot of yard work.

A friend of mine, Luck Henson, was still walking around a track most days on into his nineties. He was stooped, held a cane in one hand and the track rail in the other, and moved slowly, but he kept right on walking and exercising. Oliver Dean is another friend of mine in his nineties; and though he had to give up tennis a few years ago, he still plays pool at the Christian activity center.

There are more striking examples of people exercising and competing in athletics in their senior years—I've just shared with you some of those closest to me. Although scientific studies and statistics prove the value of exercise, I have chosen to give you personal testimony and observations about the benefits of exercise during the retirement years.

Nourish the Body

A Changing Diet

As we move on in retirement we may have to give up a lot of activities we once enjoyed; but we never retire from eating. I read that the body is an autobiography of a person's life. Whether this is true or not, I don't know. But the body does tend to reflect a lifetime of exercise and eating habits. And the diet most prescribed for retirees likely calls for a radical change in food selection. Mark Twain caused Pudd'nhead Wilson to say, "The only way to keep your health is to eat what you don't want, drink what you don't like, and do what you'd rather not." Giving up sugar, fat, salt, and cholesterol may take much of the flavor out of eating and the enjoyment out of what we like to taste. But I believe there's a sensible approach that balances a changing diet with a continuing appetite for what we like to eat.

Learn What's Best

Doctors, dieticians, and wise laypersons can identify the kind of diet that best contributes to good health and longevity. Most of us share some ignorance about the kind of diet that is best for us. Oh, we may know that we need to cut down on fat, reduce the salt, and watch the calories. But we may not be aware that canned soups contain a lot of salt. We may not know the difference between saturated and unsaturated fats. The event of a heart attack or some other condition is a hard way to learn an easy lesson. A part of good stewardship of life is to learn what is best for us to eat and to make healthy eating a part of our lifestyles.

Appetites and Aberrations

Normally we eat healthy at our house. That's mainly because Phyllis prepares broccoli, cauliflower, asparagus, and other vegetables that I would never bring home from the grocery store. She offers me lots of opportunities to eat fruits, which I do enjoy. But she also has the wisdom to know that a steady diet of healthy food doesn't satisfy some of our lifetime appetites and longings.

So occasionally we enjoy an aberration that departs from our healthy diet. One morning as I was shaving, I smelled the aroma of what I knew had to be a wonderful aberration: sausage cooking, the aroma of eggs mingled with onions and peppers in preparation, grits being stirred, biscuits in the oven, and the scent of "leaded" coffee. We ate like there would be no tomorrow. If we ate this way every day, there would indeed be no tomorrow! But the next day it was back to bagels, cereal, and the like.

Tasty, Healthful Foods

One of the benefits of modern technology is that we're beginning to have more and more foods that are both healthful and tasty. I've been wowed with fat-free potato chips. Decaffeinated coffee has reached a new plateau of taste. Some sandwiches and other foods have just a few fat grams and not too many calories. So it's possible to enjoy a healthy diet that keeps tabs on fat, calories, sodium, and cholesterol without becoming paranoid or obnoxious to others about your menu.

Eating and Abstaining

It's been said that some people live to eat, while others eat to live. In retirement, it's not enough to know what to eat and what not to eat. We need to know *when* to eat and when not to eat. Nourishing the body calls for eating regular meals, but it also calls for abstaining from recreational eating. One extreme we sometimes see in retirement is the loss of appetite and a carelessness about eating enough to nourish the body. Another extreme is to eat recreationally as a pastime, filling your body when you're not even hungry and adding fat when you could do with less weight. Most of our adult lives, Phyllis and I have weighed ourselves every day. I record her weight and mine in my daily diary. The number of pounds we weigh usually affects the choice and quantity of what we eat each day. We have an overall commitment to keep from ballooning up in weight.

Our goal is to nourish the body while eating wisely.

The Soul Connection

An itinerant evangelist of another era worked himself to death. As he lay dying, he was heard to say that he had "killed the horse, which must carry the mail." My Uncle Charlie Aiken put it another way. At age seventy-eight, dealing with surgeries that came in staccato sequence, he said, "I was busy keeping my mind in order, and my body fell apart." These two observations summarize what you've just read. Going back to our opening quote, "The human body is an instrument for the production of the human soul." Be sure that you make this body-soul connection.

In retirement, most of us can improve or maintain our health. We owe it to our souls to take good care of our bodies and to use them well.

◄ *Reflections*

- Consider to what extent this statement applies to you: "If I had known I was going to live this long, I would have taken better care of my body."

- Apply one of the three following grades to each decade of your life so far: good, bad, so-so. (Or, pencil-and-paper a decade-by-decade health time line of your life in these terms.)

- What could you possibly have done to improve the "bad" or "so-so" to "good"?

- What personal choices have most hurt your body? helped your body?

- If you were talking to a doctor, how would you describe your health now?

Projections ➤

- Complete this sentence: "As I grow older, I will stay young by …"

- Write on a calendar the date by which you will have completed this year's physical (including mammogram or prostate check), dental exam, and eye checkup.

- Choose one exercise your doctor approves for you to do daily (for example, walk a mile or stretch your limbs for a few minutes).

- Weigh yourself today, write down your weight, and commit that you will not gain a pound this year—unless you need to gain weight.

- What would it take to begin eating what is best for your body?

Retirement Words from The Word

" 'Please test your servants for ten days: Give us nothing but vegetables to eat and water to drink.'... At the end of the ten days they looked healthier and better nourished than any of the young men who ate the royal food" (Dan. 1:12,15).

"Do not worry about your life, what you will eat, or about your body, what you will wear. For life is more than food, and the body more than clothing" (Luke 12:22–23, NRSV).

"Cast all your anxiety on him, because he cares for you" (1 Peter 5:7, NRSV).

"Do you not know that your body is a temple of the Holy Spirit, who is in you, whom you have received from God? You are not your own; you were bought at a price. Therefore honor God with your body" (1 Cor. 6:19–20).

Prayer

Father, thank You for the
gift of my body and all that nourishes
and sustains it. May I not give up on
my earthly body before I finish doing
what You have called me to do with it.
Help me renew my commitment to
be a good steward of my body
and to turn all of my anxieties
about it over to You.
Amen.

8

...Soul

All great art is the work of the whole living creature,
body and soul, and chiefly of the soul.
—John Ruskin

Actually, body and soul go together, so this chapter is a continuation of the last chapter. However, the focus on soul ascends to a higher level of personhood than what you've just read about the body, which wears out and dies. The soul is created within time but does not end in all eternity. And though the soul may grow weary, it need not deteriorate or become less than what it has been. In fact, as Hippocrates said, "The human soul develops up to the time of death."

I would add that there is no evidence that the human soul quits developing even at death. Rather, I agree with Goethe, who wrote, "I am fully convinced that the soul is indestructible, and that its activity will continue through eternity. It is like the sun, which, to our eyes, seems to set in night; but it has in reality only gone to diffuse its light elsewhere."

Getting a Handle on "Soul"

It's hard to get a handle on what the word *soul* means. There are many different viewpoints about what a soul is. Without claiming to be a philosopher or a theologian, let me explain where I'm coming from as I speak of soul. Otherwise we might not be reading from the same page, so to speak.

For me, the word soul refers to all that's involved in ongoing personhood: the total being. When I speak of soul, I mean the heart, mind, spirit, intellect, will, emotions, vitality, and person clothed in a recognizable body—both in this life and beyond. Body and soul make up the whole person. Even when the earthly body and soul are separated by death, I believe God provides a body fit for all eternity. (See 2 Corinthians 4:14–5:10.) Theologian Christian Wolf wrote, "A person is not at any time viewed as a bodyless soul."

Claude Hailey, a friend of mine, owns a 1965 Chevelle. I was able to recognize the model without Claude identifying the car for me. However, this 1965 Chevrolet is in far better shape now than when it came off the assembly line. Claude found the car fifteen years ago, sitting in a field with a "For Sale—$200" sign on it. Since then Claude has sandblasted and rebuilt the car from the ground up, using premium parts and applying chrome to the engine and a polished finish to the body. He still works on improving this car every day. The Chevelle has won numerous trophies in car shows. Claude's car is better than it ever was before he got hold of it. I like to think that this is just a pale comparison of the difference between our bodies on earth and the resurrection bodies God has for us. And I can't imagine God doing less for our minds than He plans to do for our bodies. We're fearfully and wonderfully made, but we're going to get even better in the resurrection.

Just as we have looked at the body in retirement, now let's look at the soul in retirement. Chances are, the retirement soul may be in worse shape than the retirement body.

Getting Body and Soul Together

I am so busy.

Wayne Muller wrote that across all of society's mosaic he hears the same refrain: "I am so busy." I've heard stressed-out people complain that they're so busy that their souls needs to catch up with their bodies. And if we're not careful, this busyness may carry over into retirement.

Don't overschedule.

A retirement cliché says, "I'm so busy that I don't know when I had time to work." If a retiree says he's too busy, something's wrong. By definition, retirement means choosing what to do with our leisure time. There is a fine balance between choosing to do too much or choosing to do too little. As we get older we should be able to say, "I don't think I want to do that." Retirement is a time to get body and soul together, to avoid the madding crowd, and not to have to hurry.

Start sooner.

By nature my dad disliked hurrying; however, he spent his working life meeting schedules others set for him. When Dad retired and anyone tried to hurry him, he would say, "If I had known I was going to have to hurry, I would have started sooner." Dad chose the right body-and-soul priority. Novelist Kazuo Ishiguro said, "It is one of the enjoyments of retirement that you are able to drift through the day at your own pace." And historian Will Durant has observed that "no man who is in a hurry is quite civilized." Whether we drift or drive, it's important that we not feel driven or forced to become part of the rat race.

Choose what you want to maintain. A hippie once said to a rich man, "A lot of stuff sure does own you, doesn't it?"

Etty Hillesum wrote in her diary, "Now that I don't want to own anything anymore and am free, now I suddenly own everything, now my inner riches are immeasurable." If our possessions burden us more than they lift us, then they own us instead of our owning them.

Retirement is a good time to downsize possessions and things that require a lot of maintenance. Every possession requires maintenance, even if it's no more than a place to put it. This is a case where less may be more in terms of our quality of life. You may need to downsize your housing, yard, garden, equipment, or total obligations. After taking a total inventory, a retiree may decide he doesn't want to downsize anything. If so, there's a lot to be said for outsourcing—paying someone else to do what requires so much time that we feel harried and hurried.

Necessities of the Soul

Thoreau wrote, "Money is not required to buy one necessity of the soul." His thought set me to identifying the necessities of my soul. I don't know what those necessities are for others, but I do know what they are for me. I came face-to-face with the necessities of my soul once when I was a passenger in a jet plane preparing for a crash landing. The plane landed safely, but circling the airport in darkness caused me to identify my soul priorities and be at peace.

My decision to be born again stands head and shoulders over all other soul necessities. It is essential for time and eternity beyond time. Besides the priority of being born again, other necessities dealt with the ongoing hunger, thirst, and health of the soul. Some of the soul necessities I identified for myself need to belong to everyone, so I'll share a few of these.

Be born again.

I've enjoyed friendship and eternal life with God ever since I made a personal commitment to accept Jesus Christ as my Lord and Savior when I was seven years old. Faith in God is a personal choice, but I believe it is essential for the soul to have eternal life instead of eternal death (see John 3). It is possible to retire—and to die—without ever having met this necessity of the soul. God loves us and gave His only Son for our soul necessity. This gift truly is free to us (John 3:16; Eph. 2:8–10). If you've reached retirement age without personally trusting God through Christ, it's time for you to take care of this supreme soul necessity and be born again.

Read the Bible.

For every major turning point in my life I have found the Bible to be a living book with a living message for me in some key verse. Here are the verses so far: John 3:16 (receiving salvation); Philippians 4:13 (being empowered); Philippians 3:14 (choosing vocation); 1 Peter 5:7 (overcoming anxiety); and Ephesians 4:1 (continuing vocation). Right now the Bible is speaking to me from the Psalms, Proverbs, John, and James. When I once tried to point someone to the Bible, he responded, "Oh, I read the Bible once." He did not understand that the Bible is a dynamic book that reads us and speaks to our needs at each stage of our lives. From my own experience I believe reading the Bible in retirement is a soul necessity.

Worship at a church.

After traveling or being away from church for a while, I miss the corporate worship of God, the hymns we sing, the friends we join hearts and hands with, the message the pastor brings. Now I'm a big believer in private worship and the nourishment of solitude. I practice this on Godwin's Mountain, at home, and elsewhere. But nothing takes the place of church. Though retirees may be tempted to give up on regular church attendance, the Bible calls us to be faithful to our convictions, to assemble together, and to encourage one another (Heb. 10:23–25).

The church remains a necessity instead of an option. Christ bought the church with His own blood (Acts 20:28). Further, we find nourishment for the soul at church. And in retirement, I find myself agreeing with Stephane Mallarme: "Every soul is a melody which needs renewing."

Pray everywhere.

A friendly old retiree, standing in front of me in an appliance service line the other morning, told me that he offers a prayer of thanksgiving every morning when he wakes up and finds he's alive for a new day. I told him I do the same thing. He added, "It may not do any good, but it makes me feel better."

I've heard these words about prayer from a lot of different sources in recent years. The idea is, whether it affects God or not, prayer changes us. If you want a quick but good biblical treatment of this facet of prayer, you might try to find a copy of P. T. Forsyth's *The Soul of Prayer*. Forsyth writes, "God has some blessings for us that we'll never receive unless we ask for them."

In a public forum a great Christian philosopher once testified about answered prayer in his own life. One person in the crowd asked him, "Couldn't all your answered prayers just be coincidence?" The philosopher replied, "Yes, but I find that the coincidences come closer together when I pray."

While prayer may make us feel better, the right quality of prayer may also affect God's intentions toward us. For example, I've always heard people say that when it's your time to die, you're going to die. Not necessarily. When King Hezekiah was sick, he received God's command to set his house in order because he was going to die. Hezekiah wept and prayed. God answered, "I have heard thy prayer, I have seen thy tears: behold, I will heal thee. …And I will add unto thy days fifteen years" (2 Kings 20:1–5, KJV).

Prayer is for all of life, at all times, and everywhere; but it is especially a necessity for the retirement soul. God can use our prayers to match our souls to the retirement stage of life. He can help us accept what we can't change and what He chooses not to. Besides this, God still chooses to answer prayers by stepping in to change lives and circumstances. Prayer is a retirement necessity of the soul.

I'm sure there are other necessities of the soul, but these related to God and our spiritual lives are essential for our soul health. Otherwise—especially in retirement—disorders of the soul will likely occur.

Disorders of the Soul

Retirement is an ideal time to get the soul in shape and bring harmony to the soul's discord. The Latin poet Horace wrote, "Why do you hasten to remove anything which hurts your eye, while if something affects your soul you postpone the cure until next year?" It is possible for the disordered soul to become ordered, but time is of the essence for retirees to make the change.

A number of years ago, W. L. Northridge wrote a book titled *Disorders of the Emotional and Spiritual Life*. Among the disorders he wrote about are depression, jealousy, resentment, anxiety, a martyr complex, a critical spirit, and fear of old age. Although these soul disorders can occur at any age or stage of life, retirees are particularly susceptible to them. Northridge concluded his book by saying that all the soul disorders he had written about can be cured only through a vital spiritual experience. He wrote as a trained psychologist and pastor. I am neither, but the experience of my life says "amen" to his conclusion.

A person can have the vital spiritual experience of being born again and still experience disorders of the soul, which are often reflected in the body. To keep a soul healthy a person has to stay close to the Great Physician. Since retirement is a time of backing off from required work and other things, it's also easy to back off from spiritual discipline and closeness to God. If we let this happen, our souls quickly get out of shape and our minds tend to get out of order. Disorder-prevention is best, but second best is returning to God, who alone can rightly order our souls and give us peace and rest.

Be Magnanimous

Older people lean toward being either sweet or sour, and the spiritual condition of their soul reflects which it is. Some of the sweetest, kindest people I know are older people with poor physical health and hard circumstances, who seemingly are in the dark night of the soul. Yet they choose to be great-souled, which is the literal root meaning of magnanimous; and they choose to spread sunshine rather than gloom. They themselves are a blessing.

To be magnanimous means to be noble, generous, great-minded, great-hearted, considerate, charitable, kind, forgiving, unselfish, and unspiteful. A magnanimous person is courageously noble in mind and heart. Such a person has a nature that is above petty feelings of hurt or jealousy, and this person does not hold a grudge. He is generous and kind in judging others and gives them the benefit of a doubt. In other words, a magnanimous person has a

well-ordered soul. Retirees can choose to be magnanimous. And they can choose to match their hearts and souls
to great needs in a way that makes a difference.

Or retirees can choose to be small-souled, small-minded,
and small-spirited. I suppose one retired husband must
have chosen this for his characteristic disposition. When
his wife was a bit out of sorts one morning, her friend
asked, "Did you wake up gripy this morning?" The
woman replied, "No, I left him asleep in bed." No one
enjoys being around petty, irritable, sour-souled people,
whose very presence is a cloud on each day's sunshine.

Personally, I've been blessed by the magnanimous and
pained by the small-souled. To choose to be magnanimous
is to nourish your own soul and that of others. As Josiah
Gilbert Holland said, "The soul, like the body, lives by what
it feeds on." Feed on the blessing of being magnanimous.

Soul Enrichment

Fire-up the soul.

Ferdinand Foch said, "The most powerful weapon on
earth is the human soul on fire." Jean de la Fontaine said,
"Man is so made that when anything fires his soul, impos-
sibilities vanish." After the retirement euphoria is over,
retirees may be in danger of flame-out. The spirit dimin-
ishes and there is no fire in the bones, no sparkle in the
eye, and no vision in the heart. While retirees are anxious
about making their money last as long as their lives, many
of them lose what makes life worth living: namely, the
explosive power of a new affection. They lose purpose and
challenge that give meaning to each day of life.

Stay interested.

General Douglas MacArthur said, "Years may wrinkle
the skin, but to give up interest wrinkles the soul." So what

kinds of things keep the inner person young while the outer person grows older? You might be expecting an answer of 101 things to keep you young in retirement. Such an approach smacks of finding something to do to keep from being bored. But this won't enrich the soul. Rather, to give ourselves to others is soul-enriching.

Live within yourself.

William Morrow said, "What lies behind us and what lies before us are tiny matters compared to what lies within us." In retirement the facades and veneers of career life begin to fade, and we have to deal with who we really are, not just what we did for a living. If you ask many retirees who they are or what they do, they'll tell you what they used to do and what they used to be. Not good enough. Each person is always becoming, unless he lets his inner being die at retirement. So how do you continue to grow the inner being, the soul, in retirement?

Even the week before my dad died at age seventy-eight, he told me, "I try to learn something new every day." He was legally blind but he listened to recorded books far into each night and shared in the daytime what he had learned the night before. Reading the Bible, the classics, biographies, magazines, and newspapers all keep a person from withdrawing his mind and letting it shrivel up in retirement. For those who use computers, the Internet provides an almost inexhaustible wealth of information on any subject a person wants to learn about. The important thing is to keep using and stretching the mind, heart, soul, and spirit; otherwise it will shrivel up like an unused muscle.

Live beyond yourself.

I've told you that Dad shared each day what he had learned the night before. This is another principle of soul enrichment: Live beyond yourself. I've known retirees who become reclusive, do away with their wristwatch, give away or burn their social clothes, and move into the small shell of living only for self. This is mighty small-souled living. On the other hand, nothing enriches a soul like investing wisdom, experience, and resources in others.

As a retiree I've taken in a lot of enjoyment from leisure-time activities: a cruise, foreign travel, smelling the flowers, socializing, and amusing myself with entertainment. But my greatest joys have come from living beyond myself and helping others. I have mentored younger or inexperienced people in writing, publishing, computers, how to split firewood, and other skill areas. I have ministered by helping widows, neighbors, family members, and strangers. I have encouraged people around the world through email and a newspaper column I've written. Churches have invited me to share the gospel as their interim pastor or supply preacher. And one highlight of my retirement activities has been sharing a message of hope with those in prison who have lost hope and are hungry to hope again.

Expressions of living beyond yourself might be quite different for you. Before I began writing today, I read a question that had been posted on a computer bulletin board for seniors: "I'm retiring in a month. Do you have any suggestions or ideas on how to stay busy?" I replied that the right question is not how to stay busy; rather, it's how to stay meaningfully busy. Or to say it another way, retirees have the task of learning how to enrich the soul. Whatever your choices, it's important to live beyond yourself. The most miserable retirees I know are those who are wrapped up in themselves. The happiest ones I know live beyond themselves.

> To live beyond yourself is one of
> the best ways to grow older
> without getting old.

◄ *Reflections*

- Recall what the word *soul* meant to you before you read this chapter; then reflect on any changes or additional meanings this word has taken on for you.

- Contrast how busy you were before retirement with how busy you are now.

- How do the necessities of your soul match or differ from those I've listed?

- What disorder of the soul do you most closely identify with?

- What are you doing in retirement to enrich your soul?

Projections ►

- Consider one maintenance-item you would like to downsize or delete.

- Prioritize your own top-five soul necessities.

- Choose one way you would like to enrich your inner being.

- Plan one way to mentor, minister, or encourage someone else.
- Decide how you will commit to keep body and soul together in retirement.

Retirement Words from The Word

"Man became a living soul" (Gen. 2:7, KJV).

"Love the Lord your God with all your heart and with all your soul and with all your mind. … Love your neighbor as yourself" (Matt. 22:37,39).

"But God said unto him, 'Thou fool, this night thy soul shall be required of thee: then whose shall those things be, which thou has provided?' " (Luke 12:20, KJV).

"We do not lose heart. Though outwardly we are wasting away, yet inwardly we are being renewed day by day" (2 Cor. 4:16).

"We know that if the earthly tent we live in is destroyed, we have a building from God, an eternal house in heaven" (2 Cor. 5:1).

"Forgetting what lies behind and reaching forward to what lies ahead, I press on toward the goal for the prize of the upward call of God in Christ Jesus" (Phil. 3:13–14, NASB).

Prayer

Father, thank You for making me a
living soul and providing a body for
both earth and heaven. Help me to
see soul necessities as You do and
to cooperate with You in overcoming
disorders of my soul. May Your Spirit
enrich my soul so that I will be a good
steward of it both now and forever.
Amen.

9

Ruts and Routines

*The only difference between a rut and a grave
is their dimensions.*
—Ellen Glasgow

Upon retirement a person has the chance to think about how he has lived life, how he wants to live the rest of his life, and to decide what to change and what not to change. While there is the need for continuity in many areas of life, this is also an opportunity to break out of monotony and to choose fresh, new ways to live. Retirement can be a time to break out of deadly ruts and begin new, lively routines.

After the euphoria of retirement is over, after you get used to not having an agenda, after you've gotten away from kowtowing to others, it's time to consider the value of new routines. Chapters 9 and 10 look at how we can live retirement life fruitfully and productively.

The Problem with Ruts

Literally, a rut is a deep track that wheels make in soft ground or wear in the ground over a period of time. Figuratively, a rut is a narrow, undeviating course of life or action.

So what's wrong with a rut? For those of us who have driven over muddy roads and drug high center, we know what's wrong with ruts: getting stuck, going nowhere, or going only where others have gone. Since ruts show where others have gone, ruts may seem the safe furrow to follow; but for those who are willing to get out of the ruts, there is a big world out there.

Let me further underline what's wrong with the ruts of life. They are dull, monotonous, unrewarding, and unpromising. They are as boring as a treadmill—humdrum, unproductive, no fun, and have no passion or adventure in them. Ruts are so predictable that they take the wonder, excitement, and enthusiasm out of life. A rut is just a grave with both ends out. This is the problem with ruts, but it is a curable problem.

Identifying the Ruts of Life

Many retirees seem to categorically equate the ruts of life with whatever they've just retired from. This may be a bit simplistic and unappreciative of what has gone on before retirement. Further, it's not nearly as helpful as some careful discernment between rigid ruts and productive routines.

Personally, I don't badmouth my career; and I would encourage others not to badmouth theirs. It's good to have a solid career and appreciate it for what it's worth. It pays the bills and enables retirement. It provides productive employment that usually includes gaining and using skills. In a work career we meet and make friends who become a part of us for most or all of our lives. In work we find meaning and fulfillment. Any honorable work matched up with a person's interest and potential is a worthy way to spend a large part of one's life. But there comes a time for retirement—a time to sort out the old ruts and choose new paths that are enjoyable, fruitful, and helpful.

There are some tips that can help us identify ruts that we need to break out of. For example, a middle-aged friend of mine has spent more than half his life in one corporate job and only recently took on another rather mundane job as a profitable hobby. When we talked the other day, my friend said, "Johnnie, I'm just burned out in my regular job. I wish I could quit it and do my side-job full time." Although there's nothing wrong with his career job, the years of rigid repetition have caused him to feel he is in a rut. In such a case, Ernest Renan's counsel might be the retirement solution: "Relax yourself from one job by doing a different one."

However, many people work right up to retirement and enjoy their jobs without experiencing burnout. Where I used to work, one veteran would encourage new employees through hard times by saying, "This is a very unusual year." Then he would add, "But I've worked here twenty-five years, and so far every year has been unusual." When I came to retire from that same corporation I could agree that every year had been unusual and interesting: a mix of good times and hard times, successes and failures, joys and sorrows, but not burnout. Despite all of this, at retirement I was able to identify ruts—or semi-ruts—that I wanted to get out of; and I've pretty much done that.

Commuting was a rut. Every day on the interstate had become a rat race around an obstacle course of construction. Most everyone on the road drove faster or slower than I wanted them to; and through signs and gestures they let me know that I was driving faster or slower than they wanted *me* to. Budgeting had become a rut as I tried to outguess the economy and build on shifting corporate strategies. I wore a suit, though I feel more comfortable in jeans or shorts. My earlier excitement in airplane travel, hotels, rental cars, restaurant meals where they didn't have cornbread, and communicating with family only by phone had worn mighty thin. I loved my work; but when it came time to retire I had no trouble identifying the ruts I was ready leave in exchange for a new way of life.

Avoiding Retirement Ruts

The "Tiresome" Rut

Ruts can be as much a part of retirement as they were part of our pre-retirement. In fact some people retire tired, they themselves are tiresome, and they carry their ruts with them at each age and stage of life. G. K. Chesterton put it this way: "Woe unto them that are tired of everything, for everything will certainly be tired of them." George Bernard Shaw counseled, "Better keep yourself clean and bright; you are the window through which you must see the world."

Some honest self-appraisal and help from friends who are true enough to risk their friendship can help a person overcome a personal rut. This challenge fits with Ellen Glasgow's observation: "The toughest kind of mountain climbing is getting out of a rut." Someone else said, "He who lives in a rut will always be narrow."

It's as important to know that you are a tiresome rut as it is to know that you have bad breath. Voltaire said, "The secret of being tiresome is to tell everything." Perhaps the secret to getting out of the rut of being tiresome is to tell only in part and to listen completely.

The "Past-Tense" Rut

Although retirees have lived most of their lives in the past, it is wise not to camp in that rut too long at a time. In Europe I've seen a lot of very old cathedrals, castles, and other structures with scaffolding around them and what seems like constant repairing going on. Phyllis and I became so amused with this fact that we began a collection of scaffolding pictures that include Big Ben, St. Basil, and other famous sites. Where we took some of those pictures it occurred to me that there's more effort to maintain the past than to prepare for the future. Retirees can fall into this trap too. If we find ourselves living and talking mostly about the past, we're likely not doing what we should to live in the present and plan for the future.

The Reclusive Rut

Some individuals who were at one time socially involved enter retirement as if it is a license to become a recluse or a hermit. They may get rid of their suits or work-clothes, cease interacting with former friends, and burn bridges between all past relationships and the present. This kind of rut truly is a type of grave. It isolates a person from caring for others or being cared for by others. No matter how well a person may have written the chapters of his life up to the point of retirement, to choose the reclusive rut is to end life as an incomplete novel or an unfinished symphony. To end one's life in such a rut is to abandon stewardship of his life, even though he will still be held accountable for it.

From Ruts to Routines

Ruts and routines may share repetition and some other characteristics, but they are quite different. Although dictionaries tend to blur the differences between ruts and routines, I'm using the word *routine* in its most positive sense, which is quite different from a rut.

Among other things a routine is a consistent, regular, patterned way of doing things. A routine provides a dependable route to a particular destination or result. It is a planned, organized course of action. In the world of computers a routine is a set of coded instructions that directs the computer to perform specific tasks for effective results. A rut deadens, but a routine enables. Flannery O'Connor said, "Routine is a condition of survival." Retirees need a set of routines.

More than being a condition of survival, routine is a requisite for productive retirement and stewardship of life.

Retaining Rewarding Routines

Alfred Edward Perlman wrote, "After you've done a thing the same way for two years, look it over carefully. After five years look at it with suspicion. And after ten years throw it away and start all over." This is good advice for discovering ruts and getting out of them, but it's not good advice for beneficial routines. When the retiree is suddenly freed from having to work for a living, he may revert to childish irresponsibility or adolescent anarchy, giving up valuable routines as well as the ruts of life. I'll mention just a few examples to show the need to retain good routines—even if the routines call for periodic evaluation and improvement

Hold on to good hygiene.

During one's work life a person usually has some regular cycle for bathing, grooming, and taking care of health needs. Upon retirement this routine is interrupted, and one may be tempted to get sloppy in hygiene. Memory of how long it's been since bathing may become a problem. My regular workout at the downtown YMCA used to trigger a daily shower. Now I have to remind myself to shower between Saturday nights. Most of us will not receive the candid criticism, "You smell!" as did one famous grammarian. His reply was, "No, Madam, I stink; you smell." Perhaps it was a retiree who said, "Instead of taking baths, I've decided to stay away from people."

Company-provided physicals, eye exams, and dental insurance may be a thing of the past for retirees; but the regular monitoring of health should not become a thing of the past. Brushing teeth, combing hair, and watching one's weight should continue to be both routine and a priority in life. Unfortunately, some retirees just let themselves go to pot in these ways.

Keep on exercising.

Retirement is a crisis point in maintaining or beginning an exercise routine. Some newly retired friends of ours have stepped up their exercise, selectively altered their diet, and lost a generation of pounds. They look great and say they feel good. They were health conscious before retirement but have disciplined themselves at retirement and moved up a notch or two in taking care of themselves. They've kept a good routine and have also improved on it.

When I retired, I kept on doing the exercise routine I had done before, except that I switched from jogging to brisk walking with Phyllis. However, I read that older people can maintain their aerobic capacity and still lose significant upper body strength if they don't mix in some weight training. So I added light weights to my exercise routine and upped my sit-ups from thirty to fifty a day. As a sports doctor told me one time about our exercise routines, "We may not live any longer, but our quality of life will be better." I believe he was right.

Sadly, though, one's clothes tend to shrink more quickly in the average retiree's closet than they did during pre-retirement days. A refrigerator is nearby for frequent grazing. With more optional time and less responsibility, retirees may find themselves becoming spectators and couch potatoes more than they are participators. John F. Kennedy said, "We must use time as a tool, not a couch."

A young woman I know is related to parents and in-laws who are approximately the same age. One of the couples has faithfully kept an exercise routine through the years; the other couple has not. I heard the young woman comment that the exercisers are like teenagers compared to the other couple who haven't exercised. The thing that makes exercise a routine instead of a rut is the payoff in quality of life and perhaps in length of life. It is quickening rather than deadening.

Continue to value your values.

The heritage of our parents instills values in us from our birth through adolescence and beyond. Then we choose our own values to go with those we've inherited. Upon retirement, we may be tempted to reduce the priority we place on our values. This reduction in values may include everything from spiritual values to those of citizenship and the integrity of personhood. The way we express our values involves routines that are invaluable and need to be continued.

Church attendance, Bible reading, stewardship of money, good citizenship, and faithful commitment in marriage are just a few of the values expressed through routines. Yet these are some of the same expressions of values that often begin to get shoved aside upon retirement. John Spaulding wrote, "Keep yourself alive by throwing day by day fresh currents of thought and emotion into the things you have come to do from habit." Surely this counsel is needed most in respect to our values.

Choosing Purpose-filled Routines

Wise people prepare financially for retirement because they hope they'll have a long life, and they know it will take a lot of money to live. Many of these same people don't realize how much time they will have on their hands when they retire and don't consider the need for new, purposeful routines to make their lives both enjoyable and productive. Aimless retirees may become like water that seeks its own level. They lack destination, purpose, goals, discipline, and the empowerment that comes through making new decisions and acquiring new skills.

Your Retirement Destinations

There is a joy in being a happy wanderer without a specific destination, and this is fine. However, think of your retirement destination as the specific purposes and goals—even happy wandering—you hope to achieve during this stage of life. Then choose purpose-filled routines as the methods and routes you will use in the days, months, and years to reach your retirement destination.

At any stage in retirement, when a person doesn't have a destination and chosen routines, he becomes somewhat like Alice in Wonderland, who asked: "Would you tell me, please, which way I ought to go from here?" "That depends a good deal on where you want to get to," answered the Cheshire Cat. "I don't much care where," said Alice. "Then it doesn't matter which way you go," said the Cat.

Each of us exchanges every day of life for something, and it is a prostitution of life to exchange it for something unworthy of our potential and our calling. Jose Ortega y Gasset wrote, "Life is lost at finding itself all alone. Mere egoism is a labyrinth. …Really to live is to be directed toward something, to progress toward a goal." Louis Kronenberger further defined our problem when he wrote, "The trouble with our age is that it is all signpost and no destination."

Getting Your Act Together

One retirement irony is the complaint of being too busy and not having enough time. This retirement cliché usually comes with a smile, but choosing purpose-filled routines can keep retirees from feeling like Egyptian mummies (you know—pressed for time). The cycles of work life have built-in routines, but retirement calls for rearranging and reorganizing how you go about the chosen and unchosen tasks of living.

More simply, retirement is a time to choose good, new habits rather than let yourself fall into bad old habits. Horace Bushnell wrote, "Habits are to the soul what the veins and arteries are to the blood, the courses in which it moves." Hesiod wrote, "It is best to do things systematically since we are only human, and disorder is our worst enemy." Napoleon said, "Order marches with weighty and measured strides; disorder is always in a hurry." And the Bible commands, "Let all things be done decently and in order" (1 Cor. 14:40).

In retirement there is time for both the destination of happy spontaneity and the destination of powerful productivity through routines of purpose and organization.

Burning Brightly Once Again

Retirement occurs for many stated reasons: reaching a specific age, personal health problems, health problems of family members, downsizing, bankrupt companies, personal choice at any age, or something else. Despite stated reasons for retirement, burnout is often an accompanying factor involved in retirement. Burnout refers to the condition of being worn out physically or emotionally because of long-term stresses and demands that exhaust a person's total being. The light that once burned so brightly now burns dimly or smolders in burnout. For the burned-out person, life has become dingy or dark and isn't any fun.

Recently I learned the word *quotidian*. It simply refers to things that recur daily—such as sunrises and sunsets. A lot of life is repetitious, and we ought not despise the quotidian cycles that give us a sense of order and comfort. At the same time, we need to be open to new experiences, challenging goals, serendipities, and what theologians used to refer to as "the expulsive power of a new affection."

The Bible has a word of hope for those who are bruised and burned out. Isaiah 42:3 says, "A bruised reed he will not break, and a smoldering wick he will not snuff out." Another translation reads, "A bruised reed he will not break, and a dimly burning wick he will not quench" (NRSV). If you will let Him, God will heal your bruises. He will trim the burned-out wick, refill the lamp with His oil, and cause the light of your life to burn brightly once again.

It's good to know the difference between ruts and routines and to be willing to explore the roads less traveled.

◄ Reflections

- What are three enduring appreciations you have for your work career?

- Identify at least two pre-retirement work ruts you're glad to be out of.

- Consider whether you have quit any pre-retirement routines you would do well to renew.

- How happy are you with the routines or habits you've gotten into since you retired?

Projections ►

- Which recurring retirement attitude, feeling, or action would you most like to change? Label it, record a date by which you intend to make this change, and map out the routine you plan to use to make it.

- Choose three destinations or goals you would most like to reach in retirement. (For example, a place to visit, a dream to fulfill, a good habit to develop.)

- What if the way you choose to live this year of life were to determine whether God would give you another year to live? How would you calendar this year and what routines would you plan to follow?

- Identify any areas of your life that are burning dimly. Consider asking God to trim the wick so there will be new light, intensity, and enjoyment in those areas of life.

Retirement Words from The Word

"There is a time for everything, and a season for every activity under heaven" (Eccl. 3:1).

"Fear God, and keep his commandments; for that is the whole duty of everyone" (Eccl. 12:13, NRSV).

"The one who had received the one talent went off and dug a hole in the ground and hid his master's money" (Matt. 25:18, NRSV).

"Anyone, then, who knows the good he ought to do and doesn't do it, sins" (James 4:17).

"Never tire of doing what is right" (2 Thess. 3:13).

"You are the light of the world. ...Let your light shine before others, so that they may see your good works and give glory to your Father in heaven" (Matt. 5:14,16, NRSV).

Prayer

Father, thank You for the gift of work.
Thank You for delivering us from
unproductive ruts that deaden
the spirit and fail to provide good
stewardship of life. Help us to realize
that retirement is not a time to bury
our talents in a hole or to fail to do
the good You've called us to. Refresh
our desire to do good and form right
habits. Trim the wick of our lives
so that our light will shine more
brightly and glorify Your name.
Amen.

10
While It Is Day

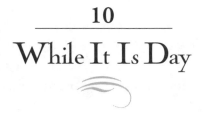

We all exchange each day of life for something.
–Johnnie Godwin

When former talk-show host Johnny Carson was asked what he would like for his epitaph, Carson replied, "I'll be right back." When we have exchanged retirement and all of our lives for something, we won't be right back (unless the Lord comes back first). The Bible underlines this fact by saying, "We must work the works of him who sent me while it is day; night is coming when no one can work" (John 9:4, NRSV).

We all exchange each day of life for something, and retirement doesn't change this fact. So how we choose to spend the days of our retirement reflects the values we hold and what we're willing to exchange life for. Ultimately, commitment to Christ is the only thing worth exchanging our lives for. (See Matthew 16:24–27.)

Given this foundational truth, we have the opportunity and challenge to exchange the days of our lives for every God-designed activity in each season of life. Retirees can be glad that God wants us to be happy and enjoy ourselves both in work and play. (See Ecclesiastes 3:1–15.)

Now I have purposely avoided writing a book about 101 things to do in retirement. Rather, I've mostly chosen to share my personal pilgrimage, observations, and tips for you to consider in customizing retirement to suit yourself. However in considering how to spend the days and years of retirement life, I'm going to make some specific suggestions that you might find helpful as you choose how to exchange the days of your life.

On the other hand, what you read may just be the catalyst that helps you envision new destinations and routines. After all, as someone has said, one purpose of a book is to get people to think for themselves. Your personhood and your experiences blend together to make you unique—one of a kind. So consider patterns, models, and suggestions as opportunities to stimulate you to choose how you want to be useful and productive.

Specific Tips

Make it a habit to help others.

In my neighborhood I've become known as the local Paul Bunyan. Our neighborhood has a lot of trees that vary from large to huge, and we have storms that tend to fell a tree or two each time or blow off some large limbs. One of my hobbies has been cutting and splitting my own firewood, so in retirement I just routinely offer to help cut up fallen trees and carry them away in my pickup to Godwin's Mountain—or to some needy soul. I'm small of stature, and one of my neighbors is a large but gentle man who is soft-spoken. One day we worked together on a huge tree that had fallen. After I'd cut and he'd lifted logs into position for half the day, he said, "Johnnie, you're Paul Bunyan and I'm Babe the Blue Ox." I liked this comparison. Also I've enjoyed becoming the Good Samaritan who helps people at the side of the road instead of the professional passerby about to be late for work or a meeting.

Usually retired people are experienced and skilled in one

or more areas of expertise and can freely offer specialized help to those who need it. At one school, one hundred high school students had signed up for Latin; but the Latin teacher had just retired and left a vacancy the school hadn't been able to fill. A seventy-eight-year-old great-grandmother had taught Latin for twenty-seven years before she'd retired seventeen years ago. When this teaching emergency arose, she was glad to bring her Latin expertise back into the classroom until the school could find another qualified teacher. Like an oak tree that retains its leaves until a new generation takes over, retirees can bridge generations of knowledge and skills.

Other kinds of service don't require any special training other than open eyes and a commitment to help. A retiree can house-sit for friends or neighbors on vacation, provide transportation for those who need it, help someone with their children—any number of ways to help may come to mind. As retirees are useful and productive, they can help others and also continue to find personal fulfillment.

Volunteer for something.

Retiree Copper Daugherty, one of my best friends, was diagnosed with lung cancer and cured of it a few years ago. When he recovered, he did more than thank those who had helped him. He volunteered to help several days a week in the cancer clinic, where he can empathize with those who are receiving treatment. He happily alternates this routine with plenty of golf, ministry through his church, and other activities that give special meaning to his retirement life.

Other volunteers find ways that they especially enjoy helping others. Some deliver Meals-on-Wheels to nourish and enable those who can't prepare their own food but still want to live in their own homes. Others take audiocassettes of books or sermons to those who are confined to home but want to grow and stay lively. Special support groups or ministries need volunteers to stand by a phone line that offers support, encouragement, and prayers for those who call in. Bringing their wisdom and experience, retirees are well-suited for these kinds of service.

Volunteering for mission assignments is a hope-sharing experience that enriches retirees and those they serve. I've just read about eighty-four-year-old Margaret Burks who is doing missionary work in Africa. She is one of thousands of retirees who take their Christian witness and a variety of skills to people who need both. The assignments may last weeks, months, or a couple of years; but God can use those laser-beamed volunteer efforts to etch His will into eternity. How do you get started? Share your willingness with your pastor, local church, or denominational mission board. Then you will enter a great adventure.

Adopt a project-oriented approach to retirement.

Over the seven-plus years of my retirement I've discovered that I don't like to commit myself to long-term projects. These get to be too much like pre-retirement work. So when I say yes to something, I do it wholeheartedly and without resentment; and when I say no to some invitation, I decline the invitation without guilt.

The value of a project-oriented approach is that it calls for a degree of commitment, work, goals, and results; but it is usually short-term. The project may be a day-trip, a cruise, or a longer journey; but it is relatively short compared to all of life. A project-oriented approach allows a person to be productive but flexible and not get bogged down in ruts. Retirees can be useful until they're used up and for as long as they wake up on the right side of the daisies. I believe this is the way retirement ought to be.

Keep a retirement journal.

I started keeping a daily diary when I was seventeen years old and still keep one today. However long or short the years of retirement are, a diary or journal is a valuable tool. It's still true that the dimmest ink is stronger than the strongest memory. And memory doesn't tend to be a strong suit in the retirement years. So a journal is a good record book to check for facts and to retain memorable experiences that our minds may no longer be able to recall.

Further, retirement can be a lot more productive if you set measurable goals, record them in a journal, and note your progress or completion of those goals. As I've mentioned, I also record my weight and Phyllis's weight at the bottom of the page, and this tends to keep us from ballooning up or suffering "Dunlop's Disease" (known as "done-lopped over"). The journal is a good monitor for other health matters, too, such as recording your blood pressure, results of visits to the doctor, and other medical information. A retirement journal helps you keep track of what you're exchanging these days of your life for. It lets you measure your real retirement against your dream retirement, and it is a tool to help you make the reality match the dream.

Recording the events, thoughts, and feelings of each day helps us become aware of what we are spending our lives on and exchanging our time for. Although my diary may be a good sedative to induce sleep, I like to think it contains matters of heritage and values that my family members might one day profit by reading. And what better place can you find to record the delightful sayings and antics of your grandchildren?

As I reread my diaries I get a sense of who I was, who I am, and who I would like to become. Recently I saw a hardback journal on sale for $2.99. It's worth the investment to buy one and begin the discipline of keeping a journal. And if you prefer to work on a computer, there are a number of software programs to help you keep a diary or journal. Try it; you may like it and it may make a contribution to your retirement life and productivity.

Make a daily to-do list.

I know I've said that we retirees don't want a daily agenda, but that is at the first stage of retirement. Things change—and we change—in retirement. It's kind of fun to list ten things to do today and then productively cross the items off one at a time; or move some of the items to a new to-do list. On the other hand, because you're retired you can just smile and throw the list in the wastebasket at the end of the day if you want to.

On the worthwhile side, I read that just making a to-do list causes a person to be about twenty percent more productive than not making one. So one of my personal habits is to make a daily or weekly to-do list. This practice leads me to do some useful things I would otherwise leave undone. Further, most things that don't make it to my to-do list are out of sight and out of memory. I might mention, though, that most of the items on my list are *want*-tos and not *have*-tos.

Hone an old skill.

One cliché says "Practice makes perfect." Not so. Practicing something the wrong way never makes it perfect. Rather, the right kind of practice makes perfect. Retirement can be a time for honing and grooving a skill that has yet to reach its peak—or at least a time of maintaining a skill. Take heart from these examples:

56 **Handel** composed the Messiah when he was fifty-six.

60 **Victor Hugo** published *Les Miserables* at sixty.

61 **Jacques Offenbach** wrote his ninetieth operetta at sixty-one.

62 At sixty-two **Agatha Christie** turned her story of "Three Blind Mice" into *The Mousetrap*, which still holds the record for the longest continuous run of a play at one theater.

66 At sixty-six **Boris Pasternak** completed his book *Doctor Zhivago*.

70 At seventy **William Wordsworth** climbed a local peak and came down with new sonnets in his head.

78 At seventy-eight **Renoir** was continuing to paint despite his confinement to a wheelchair by rheumatoid arthritis.

80 At eighty **George Bernard Shaw** gave up driving but continued to walk up to six miles at a stretch.

81 At eighty-one **Henri Matisse** completed decorating a Dominican chapel.

82 At eighty-two **Goethe** completed his masterpiece *Faust*.

83 At eighty-three **Horowitz** played the piano in Carnegie Hall.

85 At eighty-five **Carl Sandburg** published *Honey and Salt*.

86 At eighty-six **Robert Frost** recited his poetry at John F. Kennedy's presidential inauguration.

87 At eighty-seven **Picasso** began a new series of etchings.

88 At eighty-eight **Arthur Rubinstein** gave twelve piano concerts in America and fifteen in Europe.

89 At eighty-nine **Georgia O'Keeffe** began a new series of oil paintings.

90 At ninety **Andres Segovia** played more than fifty concerts on his classical guitar.

91 At ninety-one **Frank Lloyd Wright** continued work on the Marin County government center and several other projects.

92 At ninety-two **P. G. Wodehouse** bemoaned the fact that he had taken up golf too late because he had been fooling around writing stories and things.

93 At ninety-three **Pablo Casals** began each day playing two Bach preludes and fugues on the piano.

94 At ninety-four **Shaw** released his final work for publication.

95 At ninety-five jazz pianist **Eubie Blake** played for a celebration on the White House lawn.

96 At ninety-six **Bertrand Russell** wrote his final diatribe against religion.

97 At ninety-seven **Marc Chagall** continued to paint and oversee his own business affairs.

98 At ninety-eight **Irving Berlin** refused to let the ASCAP (a music association) honor him with a full-page advertisement in the *New York Times*.

98 At ninety-eight **Eubie Blake** was still accepting paying gigs.

A friend of mine was a competent sales manager who was burned out from pressure to reach almost impossible sales goals. He was downsized but decided to continue using his sales ability in another field. He got his real estate license and began to sell houses. He's happier and more relaxed now than I've ever seen him, and he says he's making money hand-over-fist—which wasn't the case when he was a sales manager.

Develop a new skill.
Another old cliché says that you can't teach an old dog new tricks. Well, first of all we're humans and not dogs. Second, I suspect an old dog *can* learn new tricks if it wants to. Further, history is full of examples of people who've learned and done new things at retirement age. I was retired at fifty-five, the same age that Mark Twain learned to ride a bicycle. Consider these other examples:

58 At fifty-eight **John Steinbeck** set out in a camper to discover America. This adventure led him to write his Nobel-Prize-winning *Travels with Charlie*.

59 At age fifty-nine **Daniel Defoe's** first novel, *Robinson Crusoe,* was published.

64 At sixty-four **Samuel Johnson** began a walking tour of Scotland and the isles off its western coast.

69   At sixty-nine **John Cage** presented *A House Full of Music,* using eight hundred schoolchildren.

71   At seventy-one **Henry Miller** churned out 115 watercolors in five months for charitable contributions.

72   At seventy-two **Dizzy Gillespie** made his debut as a dramatic actor.

74   Although **William Carlos Williams** was a medical doctor for more than forty years, at age seventy-four he completed his best-known poem, "Paterson."

76   At seventy-six **Grandma Moses** gave up embroidery because of arthritis and began to paint.

79   At seventy-nine **Grandma Moses** had her first show of art in New York City.

100   At one hundred **Grandma Moses** went back to work and completed twenty-five more paintings.

101+   For those over one hundred: **The Delaney sisters** published a book about their first hundred years and then did a follow-up volume.

On a personal note, with much less grandeur than what you've just read, I've taken up a few new activities in my retirement. I have researched vacuum cleaners, bought a good one, and become a skilled vacuumer. I've used the Internet to become an amateur travel expert—using the term "expert" loosely. And although writing and publishing made up the primary context for my working career, up to the time of my retirement I had never realized my dream of writing a newspaper column. Now I have.

For the past four years I've written a weekly column called "Words and Things." Writing this newspaper column has honed and sharpened my writing skills. One goal I've not yet reached, however, is my ambition to play a harmonica well enough that others can recognize the tunes.

Marie von Ebner-Eschenbach said, "You will stay young as long as you learn, form new habits, and don't mind being contradicted." I would add the ingredient of curiosity. The curious never get bored to death, and they reveal that youth is more a matter of the heart than of the calendar. But to get real experience into the picture, let's read what Sarah and Elizabeth Delaney had to say when Sarah was 105 and Elizabeth was 103: "Most folks think getting older means giving up, not trying anything new. Well, we don't agree with that. As long as you can see each day as a chance for something new to happen, something you never experienced before, you will stay young."

Consider getting and using a computer.

Chances are you already have a computer. If not, you're probably turned off by this suggestion. Aware of this, I started to leave out this suggestion; but the potential for enriching your retirement through a computer is too great to dismiss. Someone you trust can make the buying decision for you, and you can buy all you need for $1000 or less. This includes a computer, monitor, and printer. A family member, a friend, or someone else can set these up to do what they are supposed to do—if you don't want to try it yourself.

Then your basic learning curve calls for flipping on a switch, pressing on a plastic thing called a mouse, and pointing an arrow at little symbols you click on. Typing? Hunt-and-peck will do. Oh, there's a little more to it than this, but not much.

The values of owning and using a computer are many: You can send and receive email (electronic mail) immediately from family, friends, and people all over the world—assuming they have a computer too, of course. It's quicker and cheaper than snail mail (regular mail). You can read or write email anytime—day or night. (And retirees tend to get some of their days and nights mixed up, like they did the first year of life.) You can quickly research information on anything that interests you, check the stock market, look up sports schedules and scores, check the weather forecast, print coupons for discounts on birdseed, balance your bank account, pay bills, make up your Christmas card list—just about anything you want to do.

The former president of my corporation called me a few weeks ago and said, "Johnnie, did you get my email?" I told him that I hadn't checked my in-box recently. He continued: "I sent it about ten minutes ago. It was my first email, and it will be a miracle if you get it."

This man who had commanded thousands was so proud that he himself had begun a new skill. And if you're curious, I did get his email.

Another one of my friends had dragged his feet on getting a fax machine during corporate days and even getting an answering machine to receive messages from family and friends in retirement. But not long ago I received this message from him: "Hello, Johnnie. We decided to get with the now-generation. We got a new computer and are able to email." He and his wife have joined the forty percent of adults over age fifty who have a computer in their home and the seventy percent of those who have home online access. My friend has reason to be proud as punch, and I'm glad to hear from him regularly. Retired friend Ralph Grubbs is visually and otherwise physically impaired, but he can work computer circles around anyone I know who is younger than he is.

Enough of the hard-sell approach on computers. I'm aware that some retiree friends of mine no longer even wear a watch. Some refuse to answer a ringing telephone and don't want a machine that faxes or answers or computes in their house or life. My advice concerning getting a computer is: Do it if you want to; don't if you don't. That's a large part of what retirement is about. (But, light-heartedly, let me say shame on you if you don't compute.)

Dress up once or twice a week.

In the big scope of things, this is a small retirement suggestion but a worthy one. I've exchanged the habit of wearing suits and neckties every day for casual clothes. So have some of my friends. In fact the wife of one of my friends often complains that all her husband wears now are "grubbies." It pleases him to wear grubbies most of the time as he works in the yard and grubs in the dirt. But his routine of grubbiness bothers her. Although I'm biased to vote for grubbies, I still dress up for church and special occasions. And I dress up a bit when I follow my routine of taking Phyllis on a date each week. Even in retirement, it's good for both you and others to know that you can still "clean up pretty well." Retirees don't need to impress anyone; but on the other hand it's nice to know and show that you can still look nice.

Make friendships a priority.

Some of my best friendships go back more than fifty years, and I cherish their golden nature. I make it a point to try to keep those friendships in good repair with calls, cards, and occasional get-togethers or visits. I believe it's important not to retire your friendships with your retirement. And despite the best promises to stay in touch with those you've worked beside or lived among, retirement calls for a special effort to keep long-term friendships alive and healthy.

Some of my best friendships go back less than two years, and some of those friends are a lot younger than fifty years old. They're Baby-Boomers or Generation X-ers as well as those of my own era. One of the well-known factors for successful retirement is making new friends of all ages—having intergenerational friendships.

I've found that real friendships are gender-proof and age-proof. In retirement I did contract work within a woman's organization where I was one of a handful of men and about the only retiree around. Still, I didn't sense any female chauvinism toward me and found a world of new friends. I mentored them and they mentored me. Now, a year removed from that work, these new friends and I still stay in touch.

Retirement put me twenty-five miles away from the site of my daily work and my YMCA racquetball friends. I came to give up this sport that I loved, except for beating a racquetball against a wall occasionally at our local church court. Then one night I got a call from Lynn McFarlin. "Johnnie," he said, "you don't know me. I'm Lynn McFarlin. I just moved to town from Texas, heard you play racquetball, and wondered if you would like to play in the morning." When I asked how old he was and how long he had been playing, I learned he was the age of my oldest son—twenty years younger than I. He had been playing racquetball for about twenty years, and so had I. So we got together and played and became fast friends. I would beat him one time, and he would beat me the next. Our families have developed a new friendship that surely will continue both on earth and into heaven.

Jia Yang is professor of English at the University of Beijing. She is young enough to be my daughter, but teaches Ph.D. candidates in China and is internationally recognized for leadership of those who are visually impaired. Jia herself is legally blind but manages well with the help of a computer and other tools. We have met only once—briefly when I headed up an American exhibit at the Beijing International Book Fair in 1996. The time we shared was just a few minutes, but it was long enough for me to learn of her visual impairment and for me to tell her that my mother is legally blind as well.

Jia asked for my email address, and a month or two later I was surprised to receive my first email from her. Since then we have exchanged hundreds of emails and have become good friends. Over a period of time, Jia began to use my newspaper column, "Words and Things," in her English classes. And just recently she prepared a supplementary textbook from my newspaper columns to be used by more than one thousand Ph.D. candidates at the University of Beijing. The most important thing we share is friendship. But out of this friendship she has seen potential in my meager efforts and multiplied them with her efforts in a way that I never could have done by myself. Friendship is partnership in the great journey of life.

These are just a few examples of the new friendships I've made in retirement. I didn't meet those new friends hanging around the house. I was out and about, seeking to make new friends and live life fully.

As you move on in retirement, you'll discover that you go to more funerals and fewer weddings. About the only good thing about this is that funerals don't require a wedding shower or rehearsal. The sad thing is that many lifelong or career-long friends die. Besides the grief of losing friends and retaining only gratitude for their lives, your friendship circle grows ever smaller—*unless you make new friends.*

Friendships old and new can be among the richest and most rewarding part of a productive retirement. They cause a person to look beyond self and think of "you" instead of "me." Friends help a person overcome the misery and enslavement of selfish living that monopolizes conversations, thoughts, and resources. So be on the lookout for new friends. Begin by getting their name and giving yours. Then let friendship flourish as it will.

Another Approach to Retirement

Good friend and former colleague Howard Foshee has led seminars on retirement. In addition to this he has spent more than a decade in retirement (or semi-retirement) practicing what he teaches. Howard and wife, Zola, live a rich and productive retirement, which hasn't come about as an accident. Rather, it has come from convictions, planning, and carried-out actions.

Although Howard loved his job, he approached retirement with an awareness that his job wasn't his life and that he was about to begin a new phase of life called retirement. He and Zola wanted this phase to include growing, learning, giving, and finding what God had for them in retirement. Their "want-tos" challenged them to plan retirement rather than just let it happen to them. Here's what they recommend:

Develop a mission statement.

This statement is a purposeful effort to get at who you want to be after retirement—instead of spending retirement in the "has-been" mode. The statement includes what you want to contribute, your foundational principles and core values, and the legacy you want to leave. In other words, put into words what your personal mission will be in retirement.

Perform a situation analysis.

Take an honest look at your strengths, weaknesses, threats, and opportunities. Howard suggests that strengths might be more free time and the opportunity to travel. A weakness might be reduced finances. A threat could be some type of health problem. An opportunity could involve a new ministry at your church. Once the analysis is complete, you can begin to develop ways to address your weaknesses and threats, and ways to take advantage of your strengths and opportunities.

Have a retirement vision.

The first two steps provide knowledge to take to God in prayer and ask Him to give you a retirement vision of how best to continue your Christian calling (see Ephesians 4:1). The idea is to envision the best future possible and plan to make that vision become concrete. Once the vision does come into focus, a retiree or a retired couple can plan steps to make the dream real and reach goals within it. Howard suggests that the vision will likely include categories such as spiritual life, family life, physical well-being, financial growth, and heritage (for example, writing life stories to give to children and grandchildren).

Howard concludes, "So many times in retirement we keep thinking of leisure—what we can get out of life. We need to think about what we still can give to life. That's where real fulfillment comes." Howard and Zola Foshee have been practicing giving to life for more than a decade of retirement.

Whether we approach retirement
with a list of specifics or in a more
systematic and comprehensive way,
we are still accountable
for working "while it is day."

◄ *Reflections*

- Moving toward retirement, what were three of your pre-retirement dreams? How have they panned out so far?
- Before retirement, what did you exchange the days of your life for? Looking back, what gave you the most value for the investment of your life?
- The day before you retired, who were you? How did you identify yourself?
- Since retirement, what significant contributions have you made to anyone or anything?

Projections ►

- Looking at your retirement dreams against your retirement realities, what one pattern would you most like to change? How do you plan to go about it?
- Suppose you wanted to come up with an agenda or retirement to-do list: Besides routine stuff you would do anyway, what ten items might you list?

- Reread the ten suggestions in this chapter. Then choose two or three that you would like to try. Or choose items from your own list. Give it a few weeks or months to see if the efforts are worth exchanging part of your days for.

- If your epitaph depended only on your retirement life, how would it read?

- If God were to write your epitaph for all of life, how would it likely read?

- Since you're still reading, you're still writing the last chapters of life; so there is opportunity and hope for your retirement to be a climax rather than an anticlimax of life. It's not too late to change the epitaph of your life and exchange your days for what is most valuable.

Retirement Words from The Word

"All of us must quickly carry out the tasks assigned us by the one who sent me, because there is little time left before the night falls and all work comes to an end" (John 9:4, NLT).

"What will you gain, if you own the whole world but destroy yourself? What would you give to get back your soul?" (Matt. 16:26, CEV).

"He has made everything suitable for its time; moreover he has put a sense of past and future into their minds, ... I know that there is nothing better for them than to be happy and enjoy themselves as long as they live; moreover, it is God's gift that all should eat and drink and take pleasure in all their toil" (Eccl. 3:11–13).

"Anyone who doesn't breathe is dead, and faith that doesn't do anything is just as dead!" (James 2:26, CEV).

Prayer

Father, thank You for letting me exchange the days of my life for Your blessings that have been greater than I've deserved. Thank You for designing life with work and play and laughter and joy. Help me to balance life by choosing to live it fully and help me to be a good steward of retirement. May I be worthy of hearing You pronounce upon my life, "Well done, thou good and faithful servant."

Amen.

11

The Changing Nest

Time will teach thee soon the truth,
There are no birds in last year's nest!
—Longfellow

The Bible often compares the home to a nest. Numbers 24:21 reads, "Strong is thy dwelling place, and thou puttest thy nest in a rock" (KJV). Proverbs 27:8 says, "As a bird that wandereth from her nest, so is a man that wandereth from his place." Jesus noted that birds have nests, but He himself didn't have a place to lay His head (Matt. 8:20).

Poets have also compared the home to a nest. Longfellow echoed what Cervantes had written much earlier: "Never look for birds of this year in the nests of the last." Sydney Lanier wrote, "As the marsh hen secretly builds on the water sod,/Behold I will build me a nest on the greatness of God." In "Divine Songs," Isaac Watts observed, "Birds in their little nests agree;/And 'tis a shameful sight,/When children of one family/Fall out, and chide, and fight."

I like this comparison of the home to a nest. However it is worth recalling that a home without a family is just a house. So I'm writing both about the family *and* the house. The home is a nest that needs fresh adaptation to each new season of life. This is especially true in the retirement season of life.

The Cycle of Life

At the risk of being picky, let me point out that Cervantes and Longfellow weren't completely right in saying that we ought not look for birds of this year in the nests of last. I asked one bird expert if birds always build new nests each year, or if they ever use their old ones. He said that birds do usually build new nests because of the winter deterioration of last year's nest and its unsuitability for the new year. However, he added that he had personally watched a robin add a new lining of grass and twigs to an existing layer of a mud nest for two years in a row. He also said that older birds are more likely to build on an existing nest than younger birds are. Reference books reveal that the golden eagle builds a large nest, uses it from year to year, increasing the size of the nest until it sometimes reaches six feet in diameter. White-throated swifts and other birds may reuse the same nesting site for years.

Although humans are sometimes referred to as birds, they are not birds. Nevertheless humans can learn from this comparison. The *normal* cycle of life goes something like this for adult humans: meeting, courtship, mating, producing young, rearing young, emptying the nest, becoming a duo again, then becoming single again. It is this dynamic nature of life that makes it necessary that we, like birds, adapt to each new season of our lives. The nest may need to be new and expand as the family expands. Then as it empties, it may need to be renewed or adapted to match the changing size, needs, and wants of a family.

A Life Cycle Example

John Godwin and Dimple Aiken met, magnetized, courted, married, and mated in their early twenties. For their first home, they rented a two-room apartment that had been servants quarters for the Haley Hotel in Midland, Texas. The bathroom was next door, in the hotel itself. On February 20, 1937, I was in such a hurry to be born that I appeared at about 4:00 A.M. in that little servants quarters nest instead of in a hospital. The Godwin home had entered a new season of life. The nest needed to expand, and it did. John and Dimple moved to a larger apartment and then bought a small house shortly before another bird appeared in the nest. After a third child was born, they bought a larger house to fit the needs of their growing family. Later, an adopted son became the last member to join the nest.

The whole story of John and Dimple Godwin and their family would require a book in itself; but for our purposes, we'll just focus on the changing nest. In time, I left for college and vacated a bedroom, a bathroom, and a place at the table. Next, my brother Bill left home, then my sister Marylyn, and finally my brother Paul. The fledglings gone, John and Dimple now had an empty nest. However, the nest was paid for, still suited them, and provided space for visiting children and grandchildren. So they kept it right on into their retirement years. After thirteen years of retirement, the duo became a solo again when John died. From the very beginning, this nest has been changing. Now the life cycle is almost complete, but not quite.

Eighty-five-year-old Dimple still lives independently in her own home. Widowed and legally blind, but keen of mind, able of body, and making her own choices, she still lives in the same nest she's occupied for more than forty-five years. Despite her children's pleas that she leave that nest for another, Dimple says, "I want to live in my own home until the Lord takes me to my heavenly home." This is just one scenario of a changing nest.

The Changing Family

What I have referred to as the *normal* cycle of life almost seems *abnormal* in the new millennium. The world has never been as connected or as fragmented as it is now. Although there is a World Wide Web for immediate communication and easy access to mind-boggling information, families often seem tangled in society's cobwebs. Families are often indecisive as they try to choose from the endless options. We face extremes that may range from golden years of retirement to a kind of hell on earth. To focus on the changing nest is more than just a chapter to help fill up a book; it is an issue that makes a critical difference in how we are to experience our retirement. The challenge is to know the alternatives, make wise choices, and follow up with decisive actions.

I prefer to let others deal with the gamut of current family and social problems so that you and I can keep our focus on retirement. However, retirement doesn't take place in isolation from society, so it's important to look at the changing family in relationship to retirement. To do this, it is helpful to focus on three factors: (1) God's retirement design for the family, (2) what's actually happening in families today, and (3) alternatives retirees can choose from as the nest changes.

Emptying the Nest

God's Design for the Family

Parenthood is forever. As long as parents and children live, they have a relationship and a responsibility to each other. Families will have crises, and their members should always be there for one another. *But the nest and retirement aren't forever.* After God created woman, He said, "Therefore shall a man leave his father and his mother, and shall cleave unto his wife: and they shall be one flesh" (Gen. 2:24). God designed the nest to be emptied of its fledglings so they could become independent and have their own families and lives. When the parents push the fledglings out, it may be a traumatic experience for parties (Isa. 16:2). But independence is God's design, and it's best for both parents and children.

Further, the emptying of the nest is not intended to be a hard, calloused experience, but rather one of love. The Bible gives us this image: "As an eagle stirreth up her nest, fluttereth over her young, spreadeth abroad her wings, taketh them, beareth them on her wings: So the Lord alone did lead him" (Deut. 32:11–12, KJV). I once wrote a book titled *A Security Blanket Called Home.* In this book I compared the emptying of the nest to the transition from winter to spring. When we think winter is over and the blanket is no longer needed, we take it off the bed and fold it up. But as the cold returns, we get the blanket out again for warmth. We may do this several times until spring really has come to stay. Our children may need to return home more than once for a time, but the nest is not designed for them to occupy forever. Although there are exceptions, the rule is that our children will need to leave and establish their own home.

What Happened in Our Family

Phyllis and I raised three sons and experienced both the gladness and the sadness of seeing them marry and leave home. In the bird world, there are basically two kinds of baby birds: (1) the kind that quickly use their wings and are able to fly away on their own (the nidifugous), and (2) the kind that require longer nurturing and care before they're able to leave the nest (the nidicolous). We had two sons who were nidifugous and one who was nidicolous. Our sons left home and married at different ages and stages, but they all emptied the nest eventually. And any returns were only brief respites until they could strengthen their wings and fly on their own. They and their wives have given us eight grandchildren, and they all continue to enrich our retirement lives.

When God's design for the family is carried out, retirees are free to enjoy and be productive in retirement. This freedom doesn't justify selfishness or an indulgent retirement lifestyle; rather, it opens the door to enjoy God's blessings and to continue His calling in new and productive ways.

What's Happening in Other Families

Today many families are continuing this God-designed pattern. But that's not what is happening in multitudes of other families. The trend has been for Boomers to marry later than their parents did, have children later, retire earlier, and often retire with children at home. Divorce and remarriage have mushroomed and produced multiple families that are fragmented or interwoven in a variety of ways. Millions of others are bypassing marriage—whether they produce children or not. Generation X-ers seem headed toward these same trends.

Many grown children are choosing a parasitic lifestyle that allows them to stay in the nest and sponge off their parents indefinitely. Often they pay no rent and spend all they make on themselves.

Choosing a Preferred Alternative

Parents have to choose whether they will allow such an aberration from God's design to continue on into their retirement. I know a single parent whose "bird" wouldn't leave the nest. Finally she told him, "The lease is up on this apartment. I'm renting another apartment that has only one bedroom and one key. You're going to have to get a place of your own." Hard-hearted? No, just loving discipline to cause a fledgling to get a life of his own.

Parents facing retirement in the default mode of supporting parasitic children need to make a firm decision: Is this how they want to live their retirement life, or will they choose another kind of life? Family spirit, flexibility, a sense of humor, economics, and serious retirement planning should all be involved in choosing what's best for the retirement nest.

Further, in considering one's choices, it's wise to avoid either-or thinking. You may have a dozen or more ways to deal with the changing nest at retirement. Both in the matter of emptying the nest and in other choices, it's good to look at all possible alternatives, prioritize them, and choose the best one. Sometimes this approach calls for plans A, B, C, D, and so on; and at different stages of retirement, second choices may have to take the place of first choices. I'll talk more about this when we get to the next chapter on "The Sandwich Generation." But for now let's think about the retirement nest that is empty of its fledglings.

A Nest for Each Season

Keeping the Old Nest

Suppose you retire in good health with adequate income and you like where you live. Why should you change anything about the nest you like and are comfortable in? Perhaps there is no reason to change anything in your home for the first season of retirement. Nevertheless, retirement is an occasion for considering your wants, needs, and best decisions about housing. Consider the size, age, and maintenance requirements of your current home.

Consider its location. Do you want to continue living in this neighborhood? Is it close enough to medical facilities, shopping centers, your church, other family members, and other places you plan to go to frequently? Do you feel safe? Given a choice, are you where you want to be in retirement? If so, stay there. If not, explore your options for downsizing, upsizing, or relocating.

Trying Out a New Nest

A lot of retirees rather quickly change their nest and its location when they retire. And many of them settle in their new digs only to regret that they've given up where they were. This unhappiness especially occurs when mates haven't come to a happy agreement about their retirement location and home.

I've known folks to retire from Hawaii to Florida and have difficulty with their new location. I've known others to give up extreme seasons of weather for sameness, regret it, and then retire *from* Florida. Still others have moved from a big old house to a condo and suffered claustrophobia. If possible, it's good to try out a different nest and its location for a period of time with the option of returning to the old one. This approach can save a lot of heartache and money all at the same time.

Adapting the Nest

Whether retirees remain in their old nest or move to a new one, changing seasons usually call for adapting the nest for best retirement living. Moving some walls and remodeling may provide a home office, a shop, a sewing room, or separate areas for TV-watching and reading. This relatively simple effort can keep mates from colliding physically and emotionally as they feel the need for solitude in the midst of so much retirement togetherness. In other words, match the form of the house to the functions that go on there.

With rare exceptions, aging calls for some changes in the physical surroundings at home. If there are stairs, it might be wise to invest in a chair device to ride up and down the stairs; and it might be helpful to move bedrooms or other most-used rooms to the first floor. Elder eyes usually require considerably more light than younger eyes for reading and good vision. Even those facing retinopathy or other visual impairments can profit by well-focused lighting and plenty of it. (AARP, the Association for the Advancement of Retired Persons, is an excellent source for help in this area: http://www.aarp.org. You can write: AARP; 601 E. St., N.W.; Washington, DC 20049; or call 1-800-424-3410.)

My sprightly octogenarian mother recently tripped on a throw rug and crashed to the floor in her home. It broke her pelvis, and then another accident in the rehab hospital dislocated her shoulder. Her family doctor said that a few years ago such accidents would have been the kiss of death for an eighty-five-year-old woman. But just a couple of months after all of that pain and hardship, Mother is back at home living independently—for the most part. However, the rehab professionals visited the home with Mother and suggested adaptations to prevent further accidents. Her home no longer has throw rugs, and the carpet edges have smooth coverings over them. A furniture obstacle in a hallway was removed. New handgrips are placed appropriately at entrance doors and in the bathroom. Mother didn't like some of the other suggestions, so she didn't take them. She's still in charge of her life and living independently. But her nest did require some adaptations for this stage of life.

When the Old Nest Won't Do

More senior citizens than most of us realize are able to live in their old nest until they die. They realize the dream that Job once stated: "Then I said I shall die in my nest, and I shall multiply my days as the sand" (Job 29:18–19, KJV). And that's a great way to live out life. But we aren't always able to live in the old nest until God calls us to our new one (John 14:2–3).

Retirees would do well to consider ahead of time what their second and later preferences would be if their nest has to change. Paul Tournier wrote, "At every stage in our lives it is important that our dwelling should suit the sort of life we live in it." One part of growing older involves getting advice from one's children. Ideally, the parent and children should agree on what kind of dwelling best suits the retiree's life. But as long as the parent is of sound mind and is physically able, the decision of where to live still resides with the parent. Of course, we retirees ought not to be unkind when our children suggest what they think is best for us and this isn't what we want. And we ought not be stubborn beyond reason, when what we want for ourselves is not what's best—for us and for our children.

Depending on the circumstances, retirees may choose from several options: (1) a different but more suitable house, condo, or apartment for continued independent living; (2) home-sharing with family or someone of similar needs while retaining a good degree of privacy; (3) assisted living, with just as much or as little help as is needed with meals, transportation, amenities, and medical care; or (4) a more complete level of high-quality care. Personal choice, dignity, and quality of life are precious parts of personhood that call for sensitivity and consideration by everyone.

Dad died the week after Thanksgiving. During that last Thanksgiving week, he and Mother journeyed through Texas and Tennessee to visit all of their children, grand-children, and great grandchildren. When they got back home and settled in, Dad got the flu and died suddenly one morning. Sometime later, after the shock and grief were less, Mother began to say with thanksgiving, "Your daddy wasn't cut out for a nursing home." In other words, she was glad he hadn't had to leave the old nest before he died.

I don't suppose any of us are cut out for a nursing home; but if we can't have what we are cut out for, it's a good idea to make our own choices ahead of time. Retirement is a time for active decision-making, not for passive resignation. Your choices are yours to make.

Wherever our nest is, we can rest assured that God's eye is still on the sparrow. He provides for us now, and what He is preparing for us is better than any nest we've ever occupied on earth.

◄ Reflections

- How did you feel about leaving home to establish your own home? How do you think your parents felt?

- Identify a past dream yet unfulfilled for the empty-nest retirement years. What has kept this dream from being fulfilled?

- Recall your favorite nesting place of all the homes you've lived in. What made that your favorite place?

- How well have you planned for the changing nest of retirement?

Projections ►

- If your nest isn't empty, would you like it to be? What plans do you have to nudge the fledglings toward independence?

- If your nest isn't empty and likely won't become empty for one reason or another, what choices do you need to make for a full and meaningful retirement?

- Describe your first choice of housing and location for the next ten years of retirement. Describe your second choice. What plans and decisions do you need to make now in order to create the home you hope to live in for the next ten years?

- If you should stay right where you are, what would you like to change to make your current nest more comfortable and usable?

- If you were no longer able to live independently, what would be your first choice? second choice? third choice? Share these choices with family and friends.

Retirement Words from The Word

"Are not two sparrows sold for a farthing? And one of them shall not fall on the ground without your Father" (Matt. 10:29, KJV).

"Are not five sparrows sold for two farthings, and not one of them is forgotten before God?" (Luke 12:6, KJV). Note: God doesn't even forget the sparrow thrown in for free.

"Which of you, intending to build a tower, sitteth not down first, and counteth the cost, whether he have sufficient to finish it?" (Luke 14:28. KJV).

"It is not that we think we can do anything of lasting value by ourselves. Our only power and success come from God" (2 Cor. 3:5, NLT).

"Do not be anxious for tomorrow; for tomorrow will care for itself. Each day has enough trouble of its own" (Matt. 6:34, NASB).

"Now we know that if the earthly tent we live in is destroyed, we have a building from God, an eternal house in heaven, not built by human hands" (2 Cor. 5:1).

"In my Father's house are many mansions: if it were not so, I would have told you. I go to prepare a place for you" (John 14:2, KJV).

Prayer

Father, help us to have the wisdom
and courage to enable our children to
empty the nest. May we look to You
for insight and direction to choose our
retirement location and housing.
And may we turn any anxieties over
to You with the confidence that
You care for us and will provide for us.
Amen.

12

The Sandwich Generation

At every moment, no matter what the accumulated ruins
may be, there is a plan of God to be found.
—Paul Tournier

This chapter builds on the last chapter; however, this chapter's development is not nearly as neat. "The Sandwich Generation" focuses on un-neat circumstances that challenge retirees and their families. I'll be repeating some things to underline and emphasize points that are too important to mention only once.

Each developmental stage of life has its own job description. When family members can no longer completely fulfill the part of life's job that calls for independent living, someone has to help them. And that someone is usually an adult child, a parent, or a grandparent—or any combination of these three plus others.

Regardless of whether a retiree is a caregiver or a care-receiver, this matter is a part of retirement that calls for active love, wisdom, creativity, and hope. And since care-giving or care-receiving almost always becomes a part of retirement, we will do well to take a look at the "*sandwich*" and the "*sandwiched.*"

Where the Term "Sandwich" Comes From

We got the word *sandwich* from John Montagu, the fourth Earl of Sandwich (a town in England). One of Montagu's vices was gambling for twenty-four hours or more at a time. When he had to choose between staying at the gambling table or leaving to eat, he wasn't satisfied with this *either-or* choice. So he made it a practice to have someone bring him a slice of beef between two pieces of bread. Hence, what we know as a sandwich was named after John Montagu in 1762. Since then "to sandwich" something in has come to mean to *squeeze* it in.

Where the Term "Sandwich Generation" Comes From

Dorothy Miller coined the term "Sandwich Generation" in 1981, and it has since become a common term to describe adults who provide both for their parents and for their own children. Technically, a Sandwich Generationer is someone who has (1) one or more aging parents who require help, and (2) at least one child still living at home. Typically, members of the Sandwich Generation are middle-aged and are primarily women. However, the Sandwich itself varies widely both in make-up and in the ages of those involved. For our retirement purposes, let's consider the context of the Sandwich Generation itself.

In the early twentieth century, most people lost their parents before they themselves had reached the age of twenty-five. In the early twenty-first century, there's a good chance that one or both parents of the new retiree are still living. The average life expectancy today is over seventy-five and is still rising. We now have our first whole generation of people living into their eighties and nineties. Couples have been marrying later than their parents did and having children later. In the last fifteen to twenty years, first-time births among women over forty have increased by fifty percent. More and more children are still living at home when their parents retire or semi-retire.

These factors have led to a Sandwich Generation that has parenting responsibilities on both ends of their lives. According to the U.S. Administration on Aging, one in four households nationwide is involved in caring for a relative or other loved one in need. Some thirty percent of caregivers are caring for two or more people, and sixty-four percent of these have jobs at the same time. Households with at least one caregiver present have tripled since 1987. Those receiving care may not all live under the same roof with their caregiver. In fact, geographical distance between the caregiver and the one requiring care is often part of the squeeze placed upon members of the Sandwich Generation.

Caring for the "Crust"

Elderly parents who can no longer manage life's responsibilities independently might be looked upon as the crust—the end of the loaf. The Sandwich Generation is responsible for its parents (see Mark 7:9–13). Those parents provided the first nest but can no longer maintain that nest without help. The parent-child fact does not change, but the respective roles change. The child still loves and honors the declining parent, but the functions change. In this sense there is a reversal of roles. All that our parents did for us when we were children we may now need to do for them. We may have to parent our parents while we're still parenting our own children.

This picture is not as bleak as it might seem at first, and I'll tell you why later. But for now, it's important to consider this factor in your own retirement plans.

The "Club-Sandwich Generation"

To complicate matters, the Sandwich Generation may find itself becoming a "Club-Sandwich Generation." The term "Club-Sandwich Generation" came to me when I realized that another layer is increasingly being added to the Sandwich. This trend especially affects retirees. Let me explain. I know a retired couple who have one parent living with them. A divorced daughter came back home and brought a daughter with her. Now four generations are living in that house. There are multiple slices of bread and more squeezing than in a simple sandwich. Eight in ten adults over age fifty are grandparents and spend some fifteen billion dollars a year on gifts alone for their grandchildren. Many of these Baby Boomer grandparents are still raising children of their own while becoming primary or secondary caregivers for their grandchildren. Instead of being footloose and fancy-free at retirement age, they're still buying kids' essentials such as clothing and diapers.

I first became aware of this challenge several years ago when I was leading a conference that focused partly on the empty nest and the possible traumas related to it. A grandparently-looking fellow in the audience raised his hand. He said, "We didn't have any problem with the empty nest. In fact, we were elated when it became empty. Our problem is what to do with the empty nest *refeathered.*" He explained that some of his grown children have returned home to live. This development obviously was not part of his retirement planning.

Sometimes these returnees are referred to as "boomerang kids"; they leave, but they tend to come back. More and more these boomerang kids are returning to their parents' nest with children of their own. Further, many of them come back to live as parasites. They contribute little or nothing. They take up space, eat up food, use utilities, and drain their parents' financial reserves. This scenario is more common than you might expect.

According to the U.S. 1997 census, some 6 percent of children under 18 live in grandparent-headed households. Further, 1.3 million of the 3.9 million children involved have no parent present in the grandparent-headed household. Although the circumstances are quite varied, some of the factors include the failure to mature to personal independence, the increase in the divorce rate, and the trend of many to mate but not marry. Whatever the cause, many fledglings return home, deposit their offspring to be the responsibility of the grandparents, and leave again to do their own thing. Or both the children and the grandchildren may return to stay for an indefinite period in the nest that was supposed to be emptied. Either way, when retirees find themselves sandwiched in this situation, they often have to put their retirement plans on hold.

Back to the "Sandwich Generation"

No two Sandwiches are exactly alike in the Sandwich Generation. But whatever the circumstances, sandwiched individuals are the pressed persons between the generational bread. They're the stuff that holds the Sandwich together. Sandwich Generationers are caught in the squeeze of multiple responsibilities for (1) their own children, (2) their own parents, and (3) maybe their grandchildren at the same time. And Sandwich Generationers are responsible for their own well-being and enjoyment.

It's possible for retirees to miss being part of the Sandwich Generation. Not everyone gets squeezed by this generational bread. However, chances are if you haven't been squeezed or aren't being squeezed now, it's just a matter of time before you will be. When and if this happens, retirees may feel they've lost their freedom. And they may find tarnish on their golden retirement dreams.

An Open-Faced Sandwich

Remember how the term *sandwich* came into being? John Montagu refused to accept either-or thinking and came up with another solution: the sandwich. If retirees are not alert and creative, they can let themselves get caught in the squeeze trap of either-or thinking. An open-faced sandwich, a smorgasbord, or a banquet may be possibilities.

Either-or Thinking

Consider some typical examples of either-or thinking that Sandwich Generationers face:

- I have to decide whether to spend time and energy with my children and mate or with my parents. Either way I'll feel guilty.

- I have to decide whether to give up things I enjoy in life or keep them at the expense of neglecting parents, my children, or my mate.

- I have to miss sleep in order to care for everyone's needs or else leave their needs unmet.

- I have to meet everyone's needs or they won't be met.

- I have to abandon my plans or put them on hold.

- All of these choices involve either-or thinking. Sometimes there are only two choices, but that's not usually the case.

Preferred Alternatives

I spend a lot of time on the Internet and I receive a lot of email. This email includes everything from funny stuff to serious stuff. Often some of the serious stuff that someone shares will end this way: "You can either share this message [as you ought to] or delete it [as you ought not]."

This closing statement is an effort to manipulate me to do what someone else wants me to do or to take on a guilt trip if I don't. I refuse to wear false guilt that someone else tries to impose on me. On the other hand, I usually take time to consider all the other alternatives I can think of about the message; and the alternatives tend to be numerous. Do you get the point?

There are a lot of ways Sandwich Generationers can get relief from their squeeze and even find joy in the midst of it. But first they have to break the habit of either-or thinking. Then they have to do the creative work of digging for alternatives and then choosing the preferred alternatives. I can't do this for you because your situation is unique, but I can share some personal experiences and also share some possibilities that specialists recommend.

My Family's "Sandwich Generation"

What I am writing to you is not philosophy and statistics without experience. So let me put flesh and blood on what this chapter is about.

My Parents

My parents followed God's design and reared their children toward independence. Otherwise, they would have crippled our lives. We all left home at different ages and stages. I left early and married early. During my years of expensive schooling, I needed to return to my parents' home with my wife and sons for two or three summers. Dad and Mother welcomed us home for those summers. Later, Dad and Mother provided a home and care for my maternal grandmother and an adopted son. In their fifties they volunteered to become a Sandwich Generation out of their love and concern for others.

Our Three Sons

When our own three sons had grown and left home, we enjoyed the empty nest. Then one son who was still single asked, "Dad, what do you think about me moving back home for a while?" I was not an unloving father who refused to do what my own dad had done for me. But because of this son's particular circumstances and developmental needs, I answered, "Let's consider another alternative." We did, and he didn't move back home. He was at a critical stage of learning to fly on his own or not learning to fly. He learned to fly—and better than I ever dreamed.

However, another son who was married and had children of his own got caught in downsizing and wound up without a job. When he asked us about returning home and bringing his family with him for a while, Phyllis and I were glad to say yes. The squeeze for them and us lasted only about four months. Then they were able to fly on their own and later soar like an eagle.

Phyllis's Mother

While our boys were still at home, we got a call from Phyllis's mother one night. She had lived and worked alone, but her anxious call explained that she could no longer do this; and she asked if she could come to live with us. We gladly said yes. The problem was Alzheimer's disease, and what began as a squeeze became a crush—especially for dear Phyllis. Later the doctors concluded that twenty-four-hour care was needed for the safety and health of Phyllis's mother. With anguished hearts, we and Phyllis's brother put her mother in the best nearby health-care facility available. And for about ten years or so, Phyllis faithfully visited and cared for her mother until her mother's death.

Parents and Siblings

When Dad retired at age sixty-five, he and Mother began thirteen years of good retirement together. At first they really didn't need any help other than continuing to be involved with all of us through phone calls, letters, and visits. Then Dad's vision deteriorated so that he couldn't drive. Having been a truck driver, this loss was an especially deep grief for him. But Mother was still able to drive, so they kept on going wherever they wanted to and still didn't need much help. My sister lived nearby and was a caregiver when help was needed. Then Dad died suddenly in good health at age seventy-eight.

Mother was left alone with a deteriorating memory and diminishing sight that soon left her unable to drive. My sister and her family had moved three hundred miles away, where my brother Bill also lived. Phyllis and I lived one thousand miles away. Mother was seventy-seven and needed help, so we siblings talked among ourselves. We felt Mother should come to live with one of us or even in an apartment attached to one of our houses—or at least nearby in the same city. But Mother was not brain-dead or wimpy. After B-12 shots and living alone for a while, her memory surprisingly got much better. And she wouldn't hear of moving from her beloved Midland, Texas, where she had lived for more than fifty years. So with fierce independence and a mind of her own, Mother chose to keep on living alone.

Marylyn became Mother's primary caregiver; and she and husband, Dave, helped Mother manage her financial affairs. Marylyn became the Sandwich Generationer, and she was squeezed. She had her own husband, daughter, and son, plus her church and ministry and personal needs. But with her own supportive family and with great love, this daughter has been the greatest factor to enable Mother to continue living independently with quality life.

Since Dad died—eight years ago as I write—Mother has had an ulcer, has undergone one major surgery, has broken a wrist, has fallen and broken her pelvis, and then fell and dislocated a shoulder. But except for a few days in the hospital for surgery and about four weeks in a rehab hospital, she has continued to live at home all through these years. She has had help from family and her community of caring friends. Someone either comes by to take her to church or she manages to call a taxi and get herself there despite being legally blind. She still uses the grubbing hoe as her favorite tool and makes do with everything in her house. When something breaks, she calls the Billy Van Zandt family because "they can fix anything." And they can.

Even now when we talk to Mother about her moving to be with one of us, she just smiles and says she couldn't do that. In Midland she has her home she's lived in for more than forty-five years, her church she's belonged to for sixty-five years, and her lifelong friends. She goes to bed when she wants to, gets up when she wants to, eats what she wants to, and pretty much does whatever she wants to do. She still beats most of her opponents in Rummikub. Her only complaint is, "I'm healthy and have all the time in the world to help people, but I can't see to do a blooming thing." Again, she often says, "I want to stay in my own home until the Lord takes me to my heavenly home." She has chosen her retirement.

Marylyn has continued to be the primary Sandwich Generationer. Others of us do what we can when we can from a distance; but with her special daughter-mother relationship, Marylyn is the one who has been squeezed the most. However, during Mother's recent hospitalization and coming home, the crush was enough for Marylyn to call us brothers. And it was what she should have done. We responded by giving her some relief as Phyllis and other members of our family alternated with Marylyn to be with Mother during her period of recuperation.

Things may change; but for now Mother is still independent and in control of her own life. If health, safety concerns, or disability change the current pattern, we will need to pursue another plan. But even then, we do not plan to move into Mother's life and take over like a bull in a china closet. We hope to decide with Mother what life's next best option is and find loving agreement in making that choice. And to this point, we're all glad that Mother is still what we prefer to call *feisty*.

Becoming the Crust

We Sandwich Generationers feel we're getting a peek at our own future as we look at our older parents. This peek may fill us with anxiety, dread, or possibly with conviction and peace. No matter where we are in the Sandwich, we'll one day become the crust—the end of the loaf.

While we retirees are being Sandwich Generationers or emerging from that squeeze, we have the opportunity to decide how we want life to be when we become the crust. We can talk to God and to our mates about our preferred alternatives for this stage of life. Although our first choices may have to yield to second or third choices, it's a good idea to plan how you would most like to continue to live. And it's good to share those thoughts with your children, who likely will become the next Sandwich Generation.

Mates do each other a favor when they anticipate and help prepare for the time when the duo will become a solo. Some eighty percent of the widows in the United States are women, so it is likely that the husband will die first—but not necessarily. Either way, husbands and wives do well to work as a team to prepare the smoothest way possible for the one who is widowed.

Joys for Sandwich Generationers

Rich rewards often come as serendipities when a family is sandwiched together by circumstances. Children get to look through their parents' eyes in a different way and tend to discover more of their heritage. Parents who were lonely after their children left home now find themselves in renewed relationships and closer contacts. Grandchildren and grandparents separated by miles are brought together more often. And when all the Sandwich is under one roof, laughter and humor may be brighter than the stereotypical gray tones associated with aging.

We can learn more about each other and more about life. Only in the last couple of years did I learn that Mother has kept a diary most of her life. And only this year did she let me read in her diaries as much as I wanted to. It was both a happy and poignant experience.

Mother keeps on cleaning out things in the house. She's been doing this for years, and I don't know where she has kept everything. But this year she brought out boxes of old family pictures, and we have spent hours identifying the people in the pictures, recalling memories, and trashing pictures that don't mean anything to anybody.

No one can put in words what occurs when a great-grandmother magnetizes the heart of her youngest grandchild and they share a moment that locks itself into eternity. I've witnessed this, but I don't know how to tell you about it.

The Sandwich won't last forever; so despite the pressure, learn to find joy and pleasure in it. Or if that's hoping for too much, learn to compensate by getting help from others and making helpful trade-offs as you continue to express loving care.

Productive Retirement

Although no two retirements are exactly the same in every way, there are predictable elements in most retirements. Elton Trueblood found himself being productive in one way or another until he died in his mid-nineties. And he remained productive despite the grief of his first wife's death and then later being a care-giver to his second wife until she died. As Elton aged and faced health problems, he retreated from his pattern of traveling worldwide to teach others. But he welcomed people to his own home and campus to mentor them. Though he was sandwiched by family, health, and aging itself, he remained productive.

Looking at predictable slices of retirement life, most all of us will find ourselves squeezed by caring for a child, a parent, or a mate; and often the squeezing will come from more than one direction. But every stage of retirement life can be productive in some way unless we give up and give in to the hard things that press and stress us. In fact—like the rest of life—we will not be productive if we wait until everything is just right. Things seldom are just right; and if they become so, they don't stay that way for long.

Thinking particularly about the Sandwich Generation, how can retirees avoid putting life on hold and decide to make the most of each stage of retirement?

Don't let temporary circumstances become permanent. While loving and caring for family members in crisis, refuse to let parasitic family members attach themselves to you. Exercise wisdom and tough love to help children become independent. Care for dependent parents in a way that won't enslave you or cause you to lose your own independence. And don't look at the present as if it were all of retirement.

Determine to be productive despite circumstances. For example, keep your identity and sanity by planning at least one personal activity outside care-giving that you look forward to each week. Reduce optional negative drains on your life and time, and selectively keep on doing what seems most productive. Being sandwiched is something you can endure and change in time; but in the midst of the squeeze, the challenge is to remain productive. Give up false guilt and unhealthy resentment to enjoy yourself for a time.

Get help for what crushes you. The Bible specifically commands us to bear our own burdens but also to bear one another's burdens (Gal. 6:5,1). This is not a contradiction; rather, it is a recognition that individuals have burdens to bear alone but require help for other burdens. We can carry a stone but not a boulder. There is no virtue in wearing a martyr complex instead of asking for help. Where there are adult siblings, it is wrong for one to be the Lone Ranger in care-giving. Where there are no siblings, it is wrong to deny yourself the help available through church, community, government, and creative ways to alternately share burdens. Family members have no excuse for dumping care-giving on the closest sibling or family member.

Learn how to provide onsite care from a long distance. Family care-givers onsite or nearby and those at a distance need to have good and fair agreements. However, if no family member is onsite or nearby, learn how to provide onsite care from a distance. The best source I've found for this kind of information comes from the AARP. This organization also provides links to a world of specialized help for Sandwich Generation care-givers—retired or not.

Take frequent mini-sabbaticals. Regardless of how great and intense your care-giving responsibilities, give yourself a rest. You may not know how to do this, but there is a way. Just an hour, a day, a week, or more away from these responsibilities can be magic to the soul and recharge your life with energy and fresh perspective.

Give up regret. When retirement doesn't work out the way you'd hoped or planned, regret is a futile look backward. No one can say anything or do anything to change the past; it's gone. The present is here; and what we decide now will affect our future. Whether the retiree is widowed, in poor health, or the children and parents have to be cared for, God has a plan for the present. And this plan calls for hope rather than regret, gratitude rather than grief.

Plan ahead. When you become the crust—or care-receiver—make known your preferences. This preparation is your best assurance for the kind of retirement life you want. This preparation will help those who love you.

God has a plan for each moment
of our lives, and He has already
planned for what we can't anticipate.
It is not just a platitude to counsel
all Sandwich Generationers
to make prayer a priority for
this special time in life.

◄ *Reflections*

- Did you know all four of your grandparents? If you have grandchildren, have they known all four of their grandparents?

- If your grandparents or parents were ever Sandwich Generationers, how did they handle it? What would you have done differently?

- If your grandparents or parents retired, reflect on the stages of their retirement or semi-retirement. What was most satisfying for them? Most frustrating?

- Up to this point, how well have you prepared for retirement and the predictable stages involved in it? Think through a checklist of finances, insurance, location, keeping your will up-to-date, and what you've decided to do in retirement.

Projections ►

- If you are caught in the middle as a retiree-Sandwich-Generationer, identify at least two ways that might offer some relief from your squeeze. Choose from those listed in this chapter or come up with two ways of your own.

- If you don't see any solution to what is pressing on you right now, take at least one immediate step to get help from a family member, friend, counselor, or major resource such as AARP.

- Project your own ideal retirement. You can use time increments of one- or five-year periods to simply write down what you would like for each time frame to include. Or if you prefer, just draw a retirement time line.

- If you could no longer live independently, what would be your first alternative? Your second alternative? Share these choices with your family members.

- When a Sandwich Generation situation occurs, what are at least two good things that might come out of it?

Retirement Words from The Word

"Honor thy father and thy mother: that thy days may be long upon the land which the Lord thy God giveth thee" (Exod. 20:12, KJV).

"You say it is all right for people to say to their parents, 'Sorry, I can't help you. For I have vowed to give to God what I could have given to you.' You let them disregard their needy parents. As such, you break the law of God in order to protect your own tradition" (Mark 7:11–13, NLT).

"Bear one another's burdens, and in this way you will fulfill the law of Christ. …For all must carry their own loads" (Gal. 6:2,5; NRSV).

"Give all your worries and cares to God, for he cares about what happens to you" (1 Peter 5:7, NLT).

"I can do all things through Christ which strengtheneth me" (Phil. 4:13, KJV).

Prayer

Father, help us to lovingly nourish
our children and cherish our parents
with honor and care. Help us to
endure the pressures that squeeze our
spirits and to rejoice and be glad in
each day You give us. We pray
for wisdom and courage to make
right decisions that will blend
care-giving and retirement joy.
Amen.

13

Retirement with Attitude

Attitude is the key to success or failure
in almost any of life's endeavors.
–Carolyn Warner

It was recreation time at the Georgia resort where I was attending a publishers' meeting. For tennis we paired up with whomever was available. My partner for the day was Tom Torbet of Appalachia, Inc. We had never played tennis together and fell way behind in our match. During a pause Tom came to me with a grin that barely covered his chagrin as we faced what looked like certain defeat. "Johnnie, do you want to forfeit, or do you want to lose graciously?" he asked. *Either-or* thinking has never been my cup of tea, and it certainly was not in this case. I replied, "I want to win." Tom kind of flinched, stepped back, and got a new look in his eye. We played every point as hard as we could, and we won. Attitude made the difference, and it usually does—especially in retirement.

The Evolvement of Attitude

About A.D. 1700, the word *attitude* came into the English language from French, Italian, and Latin to express a person's manner of feeling, thinking, posture, fitness, and disposition. Sometimes the early English spelled "attitude" as "aptitude," which comes from the

Latin spelling and originally meant likelihood or disposition. So the words *attitude* and *aptitude* have been closely related from the beginning. In other words, what we *do* is closely related to our *attitude*. And the habitual attitudes we have in retirement will largely determine our retirement enjoyment and success—or our misery and defeat.

In recent years the word *attitude* has taken on some relatively new meanings. One newer meaning of the word is to have an assertive or arrogant state of mind, a testy or uncooperative disposition. Not long ago I heard this usage when a customer couldn't get the best of a sales clerk. He said, "That's just what we need: a sales clerk with an attitude."

Another more recent shade of meaning for *attitude* is that of having the right stance in a spirited manner. I'll illustrate. A while back I was visiting a dude ranch near Scottsdale, Arizona, with a bunch of other city dudes who usually wore suits. We were gathered outside with a mix of cowboys and cowgirls for a western cookout and recreation. One of the planned activities was for experts to teach us how to line dance. Being a Baptist minister, I didn't know how to square dance. Nevertheless, I shyly gave it a polite try. One of the expert line dancers noticed that I have two left feet and that I was kind of backward in my efforts. She told me I needed to have an attitude if I was going to line dance correctly. She meant that I needed to let my hair down, get with the program, strut my stuff, and not worry about what anyone thought if I was going to get any enjoyment out of the activity. She meant that my attitude needed to be spirited, not passive. I've still got two left feet, but boy did I ever have fun when my attitude changed.

And that's what this chapter is all about.

Don't Be Crusty

In the last chapter, you will remember that I talked about the Sandwich Generation and about retirees eventually becoming the crust—the end of the loaf. If we live long enough, it's inevitable that we will become the crust. But this is no excuse for becoming crusty in our attitude.

Retirees may have lived a lifetime of statesmanship and good etiquette, often having to disguise their real attitudes. That's part of the politeness of life. Rather than hypocrisy, it's often just good sense and good business to curb the expression of attitudes that won't help and are likely to hinder. But many folks seem to feel that retirement and old age provide a license for being frank and candid—which often translates into being brutally frank and cuttingly candid. No one likes being around a person with an acrid attitude and speech that cuts like acid.

So it's good to sort out our attitudes to decide which ones we'll live by in our retirement. As Paul Tournier wrote, "A person's characteristics tend to become more accentuated as his life goes on." He added, "Therefore, if one's old age is to be happy, there must be a change of attitude."

Bypass Self-Pity

When retirees are not the Sandwich Generation, they may adopt an attitude of self-pity and throw regular pity parties for themselves. This tends to happen when the children grow up, empty the nest, move off, and have a life of their own. They're in the midst of busy careers, raising their own kids, and doing things with their immediate family. Our children may not call, write, or visit often enough to suit us retired parents. In our solitude, we may begin to feel and act sorry for ourselves. And when we do have contact with our children we may lay a false guilt trip on them and spoil the contact. This is a destructive and self-defeating attitude that retirees need to recognize and avoid. Whiny, wimpy retirees face the challenge of getting outside themselves and helping others. It's hard to feel self-pity when you're helping those who are far worse off than you.

Besides all that, there is the possibility that older parents may live longer if they don't devote themselves only to their own children. I learned this from a German study of male senior citizens. Those male senior citizens whose lives revolved around the success or social support of their own children died four years sooner than those who had friends and interests reaching beyond their children. Now I don't know whether this applies to women. But either way it's emotionally healthy to have a range of relationships that includes intergenerational friendships and is not confined to one's family. Someone has said that we need old friends to grow old with and new friends to keep us young.

If pity is one of our attitudes, we would do well to direct it toward those who deserve it rather than toward ourselves.

Retreat from Resentment

Few people reach retirement age without having been slighted, insulted, mistreated, or injured in some way that can result in resentment. This attitude of ill will and negative feelings gnaws its way back into my life like a recurring ulcer from time to time. I hear a person's name and am reminded of a hurtful experience, or just find myself letting the devil replay a past resentment. However, I don't engage resentment for long but retreat from it to more positive attitudes.

When I become conscious of creeping resentment I don't treat the symptoms with an emotional Rolaid; rather, I try to go back to the cause of the resentment and root it out.

This is easier said than done. I find help in Lucille T. Wessmann's counsel: "If at all possible, don't cut your bridges to what you've done and where you've been." I recall the treasure of my work years, enjoy remembering my colleagues, breathe a prayer of goodwill for those who wronged me or just rubbed me the wrong way; and I wish the best for those who succeeded me. I haven't burned any bridges of relationships nor let resentment shut a door to return visits, mental or literal.

Your resentments are your own, but they'll own you and your retirement if you entertain them for long. So it's a good idea to retreat from resentment.

Look Away from Regret

Regret is a futile focus on an unchangeable past. Regret looks at some negative thing done or undone in the past and results in present pain and remorse. Retirement provides both time and occasion for regret. Family and friends may have died before we made peace with them or shared something in our heart. Arthur Hopkins said, "There is a wealth of unexpressed love in the world. It is one of the chief causes of sorrow evoked by death: what might have been said or done that never can be said or done." Despite the truth of this statement, regret won't help one bit.

And in a similar way, regret won't help change any other area of life's past tenses. The talent or skill we didn't develop won't be developed by looking backward. The stock or real estate investment that would have made us rich or prosperous is hindsight that is usually better than foresight. No one can change the past except historians; and they do it by accident, ignorance, or deceit.

Helen Keller pointed to a better way and better attitude. She said, "When one door of happiness closes, another opens; but often we look so long at the closed door that we do not see the one which has been opened for us." This woman who was blind was able to see that we need to look away from regret and forward to possibilities.

Get Over Grief

When a mate or another loved one dies, lingering grief can freeze or end the effective life of a survivor. Most of us have seen someone who has given in to unending grief. A child may die, and the parent may preserve everything of the child's except the life of the parent. Though time goes on, the parent really doesn't go on but exists in a frozen past. When mates are close and one of them dies, the other may be grieved to death or fail to get over grief and start a new life.

Even though resurrection is a promise and a certainty, I would not minimize the need to grieve. Grief is a natural attitude of hurt that we will experience and then need to be healed of. In the Bible Naomi lost her husband and two sons. When she returned from Moab to Bethlehem her grief was so great that she changed her name from Naomi, meaning "my pleasantness," to *Mara*, which means "bitterness" (Ruth 1:19–20). Life's happiness seemingly was over for Naomi. But after Boaz married Ruth and she bore a son named Obed, Naomi was reassured: " 'May he also be to you a restorer of life and a sustainer of your old age; for your daughter-in-law, who loves you and is better to you than seven sons, has given birth to him.' Then Naomi took the child and laid him in her lap, and became his nurse" (Ruth 4:15–16). Naomi's bitterness departed and her joy in life returned—full circle.

If statistics continue in their present trend, about eighty percent of female retirees will become widows; and about twenty percent of male retirees will become widowers. It is important to grieve when this happens, but it is equally important to get over grief; for there may yet be a generation of years of productive living for the survivor.

Defeat Depression

Depression is an attitude of gloom, doom, and darkness. It's kin to grief, but there may or may not be an apparent reason for feeling so down and dismal. Besides obvious factors that plunge a person into depression, the medical community knows that a hormonal imbalance can be involved in depression. There are helpful medications for depression, and good counseling can often get at the causes and cures of depression.

Although I'm not a medical doctor or a psychologist, I'm acquainted with depression; and I know that it often accompanies retirement. Further, sooner or later, retirement offers occasion for depression. For example, an uncle of mine lived until his early eighties and experienced a decline of health that pretty much reduced his enjoyable activities to eating and watching TV. When I visited him he told me with anguish, "I used to be able to do everything; now I can't do anything." He didn't live long after that. When I spoke on a Sunday morning to a group of patients in a rehab hospital, I met a legless man who was younger than my uncle but was unable to do much more than my uncle had been able to do. Somehow, though, this man had learned to give thanks for his blessings, rather than grieve over what he had lost. Judith M. Knowlton captures the difference with this statement: "I discovered I always have choices and sometimes it's only a choice of attitude."

During my years of schooling I pushed myself day and night until my body rebelled and my spirit crashed in depression. For me, the sun wouldn't come up; and nothing anyone could say or do brought any sunshine into my life. My Christian doctor told me that I had a physical problem, not a faith problem. Over a summer, with rest and the medication of a newly discovered antidepressant, I got up one day and discovered the sun was still shining. My family was well, the birds were singing, and nature was reflecting God's artistry. For the life of me I couldn't figure out why I had been depressed, but I determined not to succumb to that kind of depression again. I put a note on my shaving mirror that read, "Depression hurts and does not help. Smile." It was a reminder and not just a gimmick, and I still quote this saying. I've been depressed a bit from time to time but never like that dark night of the soul when I was a young man.

All of this is simply to say that I know something about depression, and I'm empathetic with those who fight it. It's best not to get depressed; but should you become depressed in retirement, use every resource possible to get rid of it. I've found help in Bible verses (1 Pet. 5:7), in prayer, in soothing music, in hard physical labor, and in medication administered by a fine Christian doctor and counselor. I recommend these same resources to you. Will power alone isn't enough to end the kind of depression I've described, but I'm convinced that it is important to recognize depression and to *will* an attitude of joy instead of gloom.

Recognize Symptoms of Age Rage

- When we're easily bothered and explode over little or nothing.
- When we're ugly or sullen because we can't do what we want to or used to do.

- When we're churlish over relatively insignificant changes.
- When our inner attitude is negatively spirited rather than positively spirited.

Moving from the Negative

There are other unhealthy attitudes we ought to avoid in retirement, but the ones you've just read about seem to have a special affinity for retirement-age folks. Many others have recognized the importance of moving from the negative to the positive. Julia Seton wrote, "We have no more right to put our discordant states of mind into the lives of those around us and rob them of their sunshine and brightness than we have to enter their houses and steal their silverware." Lydia M. Child said, "You find yourself refreshed by the presence of cheerful people. Why not make an honest effort to confer that pleasure on others? Half the battle is gained if you never allow yourself to say anything gloomy." Psychologist William James wrote, "The greatest discovery of my generation is that a human being can alter his life by altering his attitude."

Accentuate the Positive

Most of us are well familiar with books and teachings on the power of positive thinking, but we may not have realized the power of negative thinking. While Christians know that self-help is not enough, we also know that in Christ we have the power to be can-do people (Phil. 4:13). It is this undefeatable spirit that serves as the best foundation for positive retirement attitudes.

A positive attitude is largely a matter of choice. People in almost identical circumstances often have opposite attitudes. This is especially noticeable in retirees. Some have an attitude of gratitude over all they're still able to do and give thanks for all their blessings. They do this despite whatever they've had to give up and regardless of health circumstances. They live life in a major key rather than in a minor key. I've observed that those who accentuate the positive are mostly those who live beyond themselves and focus on others.

As Rick Bryan states in *The Cynic's Dictionary*, the cynic looks upon retirement as "the liberation of a captive butterfly just as its wings begin to crumble." The positive realist doesn't deny a decline in health or abilities but chooses to focus on the liberation of retirement.

My mother is eighty-five, and her laughter has never been purer than it is now. She's been to sorrow and back many times; but her visits to joy and laughter seem more frequent—or more accented in her eighties. She doesn't fear what she can lose or linger in grief over what she's lost. She gives thanks; she enjoys life. She accentuates the positive.

Age with Grace

For a long time I've heard people talk about aging gracefully, and I suppose I equated this with being placid, if not passive. This has never appealed to me. But at the heart of the word *grace* is a blend of love, kindness, and active goodwill. It is in this sense that grace merits commendation as a retirement attitude. Jesus, more than anyone else, lived life with an attitude of grace as well as providing saving grace for us. And Paul was inspired to write, "Your attitude should be the same as that of Christ Jesus" (Phil. 2:5). Jesus' attitude was one of active grace as He determined to do the will of the Father.

Grace is also kin to joy. And when people age gracefully, they have a gladness, a poise, and a dignity about them that is admirable. They and their attitudes are master over life and all its circumstances. They seem to hear and obey an eleventh commandment, "Thou shalt not whine."

Those with grace have a maturity about them that matches their retirement years. I read somewhere that growing older is inevitable, but growing up is optional. This is a simple way of saying what psychologists have taught us for years: Reaching maturity is a developmental task—a job—for each stage of life. Those who age gracefully are not childish retirees, but that doesn't mean they're wooden or lacking in fun.

Discover Patience

When most people think of "the patience of Job," I suppose they still think Job was calm and imperturbable in the midst of his troubles. This isn't true; he was anguished. "The patience of Job" refers to the endurance of Job. And one of the key attitudes of retirees to choose and hang on to is the kind of patience that endures hardship. Winston Churchill reportedly gave the shortest commencement speech on record to a group of graduates. He got up to speak and said, "Never, never, never, never give up," and then he sat down. The same counsel is vital for retirees as they move through life's last chapters if they are to be the best chapters.

One retiree who had this enduring attitude fell and injured herself badly. After weeks in a rehab hospital and a setback while there, she was heard to say, "I feel like going home and just giving up." She almost lost the patience that endures, but she hung on; and she recovered from her injuries. She's still in charge of her life, which has a lot of quality left in it. And she likely won't surrender her enduring patience until it's time to surrender this life for the next.

The more traditional understanding of patience is also important in retirement. Someone defined this kind of patience as having something to do while you wait. This works for me. One car manufacturer has noted that the average person spends six months of his life in his car waiting for red lights to turn green. The point of this ad is to focus on the enjoyable surroundings within the car and the fine sound system that could even make waiting on a red light an enjoyable experience. Retirees are usually not people in authority regardless of what authority or power they wielded before retirement. They find themselves frustrated by delays in most everything—red tape in government paperwork, red lights, or insurance matters—and it may seem that nothing happens quickly, easily, or on time anymore. Having something to do while you wait is an important factor in retirement patience. Such an attitude and approach is a gift to the body, mind, and soul. Blood pressure, peace of mind, and heart disease all tend to improve with an attitude of patience.

Live with Hope

When our oldest son, Mark, married Pam, they were both working and able to buy a starter house not far from us. When we went over to see their house, Pam was proud to show us through it room by room. In the guest bedroom we saw two twin beds with a plaque over each. One plaque read "Faith," and the other read "Love." Being of a theological bent, I asked, "Where is *Hope*"? Pam answered, "They don't come in *Hope*; they just come in *Faith* and *Love.*" I smiled, but her answer stayed with me: *They don't come in Hope.*

I've found that a lot of people are asking where hope is, and many retirees seem to think that retirement doesn't come in hope. But I'm here to tell you that all of life—and especially retirement—can have hope.

Many think of hope as a wish tinged with optimism. However the New Testament states that hope is not a wish but a certainty for those who know Christ as Lord and Savior. The apostle Paul stated this plainly to those who had been hopelessly lost but had become Christians with hope. He wrote, "At that time ye were without Christ, ... having no hope, and without God in the world; but now in Christ Jesus ye ... are made nigh by the blood of Christ" (Eph. 2:12–13, KJV). Apart from the God-directed life, there is no reason to hope (Eccl.1:2). Paul further wrote, "To whom God would make known what is the riches of the glory of this mystery; ...which is Christ in you, the hope of glory" (Col.1:27, KJV).

This Christian attitude of hope is rooted in eternity, gives power for the present, and guarantees that things will get better. When I used to tell Phyllis things would get better and they didn't, she would add "in heaven." The Christian lives with the hope that things will get better on earth; but if not, the Christian lives with the certainty of hope that things will be better in heaven. Paul wrote, "According to my earnest expectation and my hope, that in nothing I shall be ashamed, but that with all boldness, as always, as now also Christ shall be magnified in my body, whether it be by life, or by death" (Phil. 1:20, KJV).

Paraphrasing and blending thoughts I've heard from others, I've concluded that hope is the music of the future; love is its melody; and faith is to dance to it. Retirees can have hope regardless of the accumulated ruins in their lives and their physical condition.

I'm not speaking of a Pollyanna hope. I'm talking about an attitude that plays the sharp notes on the keyboard of life rather than the flat notes, and the basis for such hope is found in Christ.

Near the end of Hubert Humphrey's life he recalled how his parents had lost their home and most of their possessions during the Great Depression of the 1930s. Looking back on that time and the rest of his life, Humphrey said, "In life it isn't what you've lost; it's what you've got left that counts. ...It was only a question of time before things would get better. The important thing was who would be the survivors. Who had the will to hang on for a better day."

Roy Z. Kemp said, "There is no better or more blessed bondage than to be a prisoner of hope." Although many of our earthly hopes are never fulfilled, the attitude of hope still serves its valuable purposes in our lives. It helps us endure rather than give up. It causes us to look for springtime while we're living through a winter. When life threatens to go stale, hope brings freshness. And it is hope that helps us overcome life's griefs, hurts, and scars. In fact, when hope grows around where we have been injured the most, it is exactly there that we become the strongest—like a log that will not split because it has grown around its injuries and is tough at that spot. I know—I've tried to split logs like this. A similar thing can happen in the lives of retirees who have hope.

Charlotte Barnard wrote, "I cannot sing the old songs,/Or dream those dreams again." But with grander insight, Oliver Wendell Holmes challenged, "Build the more stately mansions, O my soul,/As the swift seasons roll!/Leave thy low-vaulted past!" And I especially think that retirees profit in having the kind of hope Bonnie Prudden wrote about: "You can't turn the clock back, but you can wind it up again."

Father Keller, who founded The Christophers, wrote the poem "Hope in Action":

"Hope looks for the good in people instead of harping on the worst.

Hope opens doors where despair closes them.

Hope discovers what can be done instead of grumbling about what cannot.

Hope draws its power from a deep trust in God and the basic goodness of mankind.

Hope 'lights a candle' instead of 'cursing the darkness.'

Hope regards problems, small or large, as opportunities.

Hope cherishes no illusions, nor does it yield to cynicism.

Hope sets big goals and is not frustrated by repeated difficulties or setbacks.

Hope pushes ahead when it would be easy to quit.

Hope puts up with modest gains, realizing that 'the longest journey starts with one step.'

Hope accepts misunderstandings as the price for serving the greater good of others.

Hope is a good loser because it has the divine assurance of final victory.

In the world you will have trouble, but be brave: I have conquered the world.' (John 16:33)."

The right attitude may or may not
lengthen your life, but it will put joy
into it. Age with attitude—a spirited
attitude for successful retirement.

◄ *Reflections*

- Starting with your grandparents, parents, and immediate family members, assign each one the dominant or first attitude that comes to your mind for each person.

- Recalling those same family members, move beyond one-word attitudes and think of descriptive words that best paint a picture of their overriding dispositions toward life.

- Among the relatives you've thought of, which ones would you prefer to spend a day with or take a trip with?

- Thinking back on your own life to this point, consider some either-or words to evaluate your attitude tendencies: optimistic/pessimistic? happy/sad? bubbly/gloomy? doubtful/hopeful? cynical/trusting?

- When have you liked yourself the best? the least? How well do you like yourself now?

- Compare and contrast the two different contemporary meanings of "having an attitude."

Projections ➤

- Assuming that you can choose attitudes that will alter your life, choose one attitude you most want to avoid in retirement. Now, choose one attitude you most hope to cultivate in retirement.

- Consider taking the risk of asking three family members or friends what they consider to be your best attitude and then your worst attitude. If you discover a pattern, decide how to strengthen your best attitudes and get rid of the bad ones.

- Based on your own self-image, what kind of attitude makeover do you see a need for? Outline your makeover plan in writing, and put this plan where you'll see it and read it every single day.

- Assume for a moment that retirement will have four more mini-chapters of five years each (*Deo volente*). What are your best hopes for each of those mini-chapters? Since God in Christ is the source of real hope, ask God what your hopes should be for those mini-chapters.

Retirement Words from The Word

"Your attitude should be the same as that of Christ Jesus" (Phil. 2:5).

"There must be a spiritual renewal of your thoughts and attitudes" (Eph. 4:23, NLT).

"It is fine to be zealous, provided the purpose is good" (Gal. 4:18).

"Be honest in your estimate of yourselves, measuring your value by how much faith God has given you" (Rom. 12:3, NLT).

"Let God transform you into a new person by changing the way you think" (Rom. 12:2, NLT).

"Beloved, whatever is true, whatever is honorable, whatever is just, whatever is pure, whatever is pleasing, whatever is commendable, if there is any excellence and if there is anything worthy of praise, think about these things" (Phil. 4:8).

Prayer

Father, transform our minds so that
our attitudes will reflect the attitudes
of Jesus. Deliver us from the apathy of
a "whatever" attitude and help us to
live spirited lives with can-do attitudes
that come from knowing Your will
and doing it in Your power. Help
us retirees to have a sweet spirit
instead of a sour one. And may we
be filled with an enduring hope
for the rest of our lives until we're
at home with you or until Jesus
returns as our blessed hope.
Amen.

14

Outliving Your Money?

We all need money, but there are degrees of desperation.
—Anthony Burgess

When my own retirement came suddenly, my income went down; but my quality of life went up. Although I was downsized from my job and the level of income that I had anticipated would continue and grow for another decade, I was upsized in many other ways. My career had been great, but it had been emotionally and physically taxing. In retirement I found rest, new freedom, variety, flexibility, and the serendipity of being productive in ways that surprised me. My financial position was not as strong as I had expected it to be at retirement, but it was adequate then and continues to be adequate for the present.

Yet at every turn it seems that I run into the question, "Will you outlive your money?" And most books that deal with retirement start with financial matters or at least put them up front. Even though I know the importance of having enough money for retirement, I have purposely chosen to deal with finances toward the end of this book. This book is primarily about retirement lifestyle. Henry Ward Beecher wrote, "It is the heart that makes a man rich. He is rich according to what he is, not according to what he has." And even millionaire businessman Malcom S. Forbes said, "The quality of life is in the mind, not in material."

Another part of my decision to delay dealing with finances goes back to something that happened once when I was in a small group discussing finances. A woman friend in her eighties, with a twinkle in her eyes and a smile on her face, said, "Money's not everything, but it's way ahead of whatever is in second place." This octogenarian's look, tone, and life actually said something different from her words, though. She was actually saying that retirement and old age are not mainly about money. She was right, but she would also strongly agree that retirees need to be realistic about evaluating their financial needs and knowing how to meet them.

A Context for "Outliving Your Money"

Although many folks retire with a strong financial base, others are much less fortunate. These extremes are easy to document. According to the federal government's Administration on Aging, one of every six persons age sixty-five or older was classified as poor or near-poverty in 1997. Within this group, minorities and older women were more likely to be poor than older whites and older men. At the other end of the spectrum, 6 percent of those 65 or older reported incomes of $50,000 or more in 1998. Others fall somewhere in between these two extremes.

The financial circumstances of retirees on both sides of age sixty-five vary dramatically. It's not my purpose to identify groups of retirees and levels of income; however, I've cited these statistics merely to confirm that in retirement, "We all need money, but there are degrees of desperation."

Without depreciating the circumstances of anyone, my purpose in this chapter is to point to some tips, testimonies, and attitudes toward financial health in retirement.

I'm neither wealthy nor a financial advisor, but I believe I've got a fix on some approaches that will help answer the question about outliving your income. Further, I believe these approaches have something to say to those planning retirement, just entering retirement, or well into retirement.

Ten Financial Guidelines for Retirement

My dad, paraphrasing Will Rogers, liked to say, "Everybody's ignorant, just in different ways." He taught me to get expert help in the areas of my ignorance, and I still practice what he taught me. So I asked my own mentor, James W. Clark, for ten financial guidelines for retirement.

As a former corporate executive vice-president, Jim was both a good steward in preparing for his own retirement and also conscientiously working to help employees retire in good financial health. Then in retirement Jim worked part-time first for a tax-consulting firm and later on an IRS phone line to help folks complete their income tax reports. Although Jim is modest to a fault and doesn't claim to be a financial expert, he was glad to suggest these financial guidelines. (I chose the number ten, or we would probably have had more.)

Begin retirement planning early. Begin as early as practical, but by all means begin specific financial plans at least five years before you plan to retire.

Analyze your current and projected financial position.

(a) Consider current expenses—both what you spend and what you spend it for. (b) Consider what your preretirement income is and what your retirement income will likely be—assuming that your life will continue pretty much as it does now. Find out what your pension plan will pay you in retirement, what your Social Security benefits will likely be, any other income you can realistically expect in retirement, and any predictable cost reductions or increases in retirement.

Choose financial goals for yourself. Enlist the help of trustworthy professionals or experienced people who can help you accomplish your goals. Those you look to for help might include a qualified financial advisor, a lawyer or tax attorney, and an accountant.

Make reasonable assumptions about inflation. Then build your financial plan accordingly. As I write this near the end of 1999, inflation is running about 2.4 percent. Inflation compounds; so if the current trend continues, your fixed-income dollar will buy about thirty percent less in ten years than it does today. Although Social Security is now indexed to increase with inflation, your pension plan probably is not.

Make a detailed list of all your assets. Then place a copy of this list with your will or give a copy to those who will need to act in the event of your death or disability. The assets list needs to include everything financial: bank accounts, insurance policies, stocks, bonds, real estate, CDs, retirement accounts, and pension information.

Continue to invest in something. If at all possible, invest in something that will make you a little extra money during your retirement. Try to put your money where it will earn at least three to five percent more than the CPI increases. Over the long term, stocks have done that and more; bonds have done so at times but not over the long term. And like investing in your children, financial growth investing is better over the long term than over the short haul.

Plan to finance twenty or more years of retirement after age sixty-five. Because of increasing life spans, you might expect to live much longer than your parents or grandparents were expected to live.

Plan for long-term health care. You may or may not need long-term care insurance; but without it, even well-off retirees can see their life savings disappear very rapidly. There are varied insurance plans available to meet potential needs for long-term health care.

Determine to live within your means now and throughout your retirement. Discipline yourself to save something—regardless of how little or how much—for special things you want to do and also for investment. Develop a budget as a tool to manage and monitor your finances—not to follow slavishly but to look to if problems occur and corrections are necessary.

Use your credit wisely and to your benefit. Buy-now-pay-later *is* a good idea as long as you buy only what you need and what you can pay for on a timely basis without accumulating interest or carrying charges. *Never pay only the minimum amount allowed on credit card debt!* Pay off the entire amount every month. The interest on unpaid charges wastes retirement dollars and is usually exorbitant.

Reflections on the Ten Guidelines

You and I may find ourselves editing these ten guidelines by altering, adding, or deleting to suit ourselves. Jim Clark would be the first to say this is okay. These guidelines simply represent what he himself has gleaned over a lifetime from teachers, books, and his own experiences. On the other hand, who would be foolish enough to argue with the counsel to live within one's income? Calvin Coolidge said, "There is no dignity quite so impressive and no independence quite so important as living within your means."

But as Jim and I discussed the ten guidelines, we talked about retirees who may lack expertise or the inclination to do hands-on financial analysis and planning for themselves.

Lots of folks just don't want to deal with dollars and cents even though common sense says they have to be dealt with.

What then? Good stewardship of our life and possessions calls us to do financial planning or enlist someone to help us—preferably a combination of the two. Although there are no guarantees about a long retirement life, God-willing a retiree might live another generation or so. This possibility calls for preparation.

Just as I would be reluctant to put all of my financial eggs in one basket, I would be reluctant to put all my trust in one financial advisor. I would choose advisors from a reputable firm and from those with a proven history of both integrity and results. I would be very cautious about Lone Ranger financial consultants. But there is real wisdom in having a trusted and proven financial advisor. Left to ourselves, most of us may be too conservative or too radical in what we do with our retirement savings. A financial advisor can look at our goals, evaluate what we bring to the retirement table, ask questions, and then explain possible consequences of the choices we make.

Depending on your age and stage of retirement, it may be too late for you to do some of the early planning called for in the guidelines. Or you may not have had the luxury of retirement seminars and early planning because of sudden health factors, downsizing, business bankruptcy, or something else. Nevertheless, most of these guidelines you can begin to adopt right now, no matter what level of financial planning or implementation you have done in the past.

My Own Financial Experience

As I've told you, I was retired five to ten years earlier than I had planned. But I didn't panic even though I had gotten a relatively late start in working toward a retirement income. In fact I was in my mid-thirties before I began to save toward retirement other than paying into Social Security. But even during hard times I became aware of the quote: "Gone today, here tomorrow." And I made hay while the sun shined on my best income years.

At the time of my own retirement I had: (1) a company pension/retirement plan; (2) a 401-K savings plan matched with company funds; (3) a modest amount in an annuity fund; (4) an individual retirement account (IRA) invested in mutual funds; and (5) a Social Security bridge until I could draw Social Security on my own.

Further, I felt confident I could continue to earn income without looking for other full-time work; and this confidence has proven to be well-founded. Although I could no longer contribute to the company's 401-K savings plan, a friend and my financial counselor introduced me to the government provision for a Simplified Employment Plan (SEP) that allowed me to add to my IRA account. The SEP allowed me to contribute up to fifteen percent of my income as tax-deferred savings. I didn't plan to retire from everything at once and have still not retired in this sense. So although I'm retired, the term "semi-retired" is more accurate.

With my varied retirement resources, it might sound as if I were rich. I'm not. The amounts I had in these accounts were relatively modest. But I did follow sound financial counsel by diversifying savings with a view to my retirement income needed. And I've continued to try to save and invest some of my retirement resources.

While money is not everything, being free of constant financial strain to meet ongoing expenses has enabled me to be flexibly productive and to have a variety of choices in how I spend my time. I find that I'm able to help others and minister in ways that I couldn't if I had to focus a disproportionate amount of time on finances. Further, I've been able to say no to job offers or income possibilities that haven't suited me; and I've been able to say a glad yes to other opportunities that have come my way during retirement years.

There will likely come a time when I'm no longer able to earn money, or I may prefer not to; but that time hasn't arrived yet. When it does arrive, I've made provisions for decisions that I myself may or may not be able to make at that stage of life. And my mate, Phyllis, has interlocking provisions that match my own. Our Christian attorney has helped us update our will—including a living will, durable power of attorney assignments, and the naming of executors of our estate. Copies of all these documents are on file with our attorney, with each of our children, and in our own possession.

We have tried to be good stewards of the possessions God has entrusted to us. And we have tried to prepare decently for the time when that stewardship will pass to others.

Taking the Retirement Plunge

Most new experiences bring a mixture of excitement and anxiety. Retirement is this way. If one mate has been a homemaker and the other one out working and bringing home the bacon, entering retirement may be an especially anxious time for the homemaker.

Wives often reveal their anxiety by saying something like: "We'll have to cut back," and "We'll need to watch our money." Others may react to the mate's retirement suggestions by asking, "We can't afford that, can we?" For the one who has worked a lifetime to build a retirement nest egg to enjoy, those stated anxieties tend to put a burr under his saddle. They seem to reflect negatively on his financial planning. These statements are like asking "What's on your agenda today?"

On the other hand, the mate retiring and returning to the home needs to be sensitive to the other mate's anxiety. If the income is going to be less than it has been in the past, it's a natural concern to wonder how the two of you will make it financially. It's good to have considered this question together before retirement; it's essential to consider the matter at the beginning of retirement. Mutual sharing about finances is helpful to both mates as they plan, monitor expenses, and move on to enjoy retirement together.

Typically many expenses are deleted or reduced in retirement, and there's extra money to do some extra things. Unless there is lack of preparedness for retirement, a catastrophic illness, or some other significant money drain, one's retirement lifestyle need not be a radical comedown from his or her pre-retirement lifestyle. After plunging into retirement for a while and pausing to catch your breath, unfounded anxieties tend to go away or lessen. Of course this varies from couple to couple and how well they have prepared financially for retirement.

The Stingy-Generous Tension

Worry about money at the retirement plunge and after can lead to stinginess among those who have formerly been generous. The reason for backing away from tithing or charitable donations likely is rooted in a fear of financial insecurity. Henry Ford said, "If money is your hope for independence you will never have it. The only real security that a man will have in this world is a reserve of knowledge, experience, and ability." Joe Louis said, "I don't like money, actually, but it quiets my nerves." And holding on to money instead of being charitable seems to quiet some folks' nerves. But becoming small-souled and self-focused is a high price to pay to calm one's financial nerves.

Another tension has to do with how generous to be in retirement. My own parents kept right on tithing as they moved into retirement, and they were generous in other ways with their money. When Mother became a widow, she didn't quit tithing. In fact, Mother is generous to a fault on her small widow's pension and Social Security check, despite heavy prescription bills for chronic medical conditions.

Besides all of this she is besieged with junk-mail pleas from "ministries"—worthy and otherwise—for as much of her money as they can get. She receives special phone calls with tearful stories and urgent needs. And she gives to a number of these "ministries." Because of my own knowledge about cross-marketing, it's obvious to me that her name and address have been sold to multiple "ministries." Mother's gifts are registered in heaven, but the responsibility for judgment lies on those who ask for and get her money and how well they use it for their stated purposes.

I suppose few of us would be conned or victims of scam artists if we had Mother's attitude about money. She got a call recently telling her that she had won a $25,000 shopping spree. She told the caller that she couldn't shop because she is legally blind and that she doesn't need anything anyway. Nice answer.

It's good not to become jaded or penurious about appeals for gifts. On the other hand we are wise to investigate causes and ministries before giving to them, and thus avoid being conned or taken into a scam. Retired couples would do well to have a buffer between them and those who would greedily take away their retirement savings. This buffer can be a family member or financial advisor that outsiders have to go through to get to the bulk of a couple or widow's savings. We can all use some financial counseling to conserve what we have for the use we saved it for, and our need for such help seems to increase with aging.

When Widowhood Comes

Couples who cherish each other and their shared years of marriage don't like to think about widowhood. Yet it is a fact of retirement and aging that relates to finances and needs advance consideration. About half of all women over sixty-five are widows. In 1997 there were four times as many widows as widowers (8.5 million widows and 2.1 million widowers). On average, women outlive men by eight years; and widows are more likely to live in poverty than widowers. So it's good to plan ahead.

Ideally, mates should have equal knowledge and say in their retirement finances. Then when one dies, the surviving mate will know all about their assets, liabilities, and the details related to their financial concerns. But this ideal may be the exception rather than the rule in most marriages.

Here are some steps that financial counselors suggest a widowed person take:

(1) Contact Social Security to apply for widowed persons' benefits, and ask for details on eligibility for Medicare or other programs that may become available—for example, prescription drug benefits.

(2) If the spouse was a veteran, check possible benefits for the widowed.

(3) Search all financial papers, files, and documents available.

(4) Contact the spouse's lawyer, banker, former employers, insurance companies, investment brokers, etc. Don't

leave any financial stone unturned. If the widowed person isn't able to do these things personally, then the one who has power of attorney or another family member, advisor, or friend can offer this help.

(5) Don't make important financial decisions too quickly. For example don't sell your house, give away large sums of money, or retire from your previous lifestyle. Financial wisdom in widowhood is critically important. Time can be an ally in delaying major decisions beyond what has to be decided immediately.

For Those Who Can't Retire

For more reasons than I know, many people feel they can't retire. They may have deep business debts, lack retirement savings and income, be experiencing the repercussions of a divorce, have medical bills, or face other circumstances that require them to work beyond the point at which they would like to retire. What can they do?

First, they may be able to retire and simply not know how to make this come to pass. The financial rite of passage from full-time employment to retirement may seem like a higher hurdle than it really is. Here's another example where good financial analysts or planners may be able to help find a way to retirement. For example, reduced income means less outgo in taxation and a number of other areas proportionately related to income. Debts might be consolidated with a reduction in both monthly payments and interest. A house might be refinanced at more favorable rates. And there are other options recently made available for improving the income and outgo balance of dollars.

Another consideration for those who think they can't retire may be that they have a misconception about retirement.

Even for most people who can afford to retire, they find that they need something to do besides indulge themselves. So they become semi-retired or do something productive that continues to produce income. Those who feel they can't afford to retire may simply need to develop a better sense of their options for retirement. They may be able to cut back on hours or days of work and approach something near retirement.

One dictionary lists the word *retool* after *retirement*. For those who approach a reasonable retirement age and are worn out in their jobs, they might consider retooling for some other enjoyable work that amounts to a type of retirement or semi-retirement. A friend who has worked for the same company for a full career has also built up an avocation of cutting grass and caring for lawns. He recently told me that he would like to retire from his main job and just do the part-time job all the time. Such a seasonal occupation would provide both income and the variety of work, rest, and recreation that I define as productive retirement.

I suggested at the beginning of this book that retirees begin retirement with a sabbatical—a time of rest, a change of pace, a change of place for a while, and a chance to do something different. Even those who have to stay in the workplace might be able to throw in some mini-sabbaticals or longer vacations and take time to smell the flowers before it is winter.

Retirement is not for everyone and is not possible for some. But the most enjoyable elements of retirement may be available to those who continue to be part of the workforce.

Matching Money and Meaning

How much money does it take to enjoy a meaningful retirement? Although there are specialists who would suggest an answer to that question, the real answer is that it depends on what's meaningful to you and how well you match money to that meaning. What does life mean to you, and what does money mean to you? Someone once said, "Measure wealth not by the things you have, but by the things you have for which you would not take money." Consider these other quotes:

Henry David Thoreau— "Money is not required to buy one necessity of the soul."

Bob Dylan—"What's money? A man is a success if he gets up in the morning and gets to bed at night and in between does what he wants to do."

Ralph Waldo Emerson—"Money often costs too much."

Patrick J. Buchanan—"To view poverty simply as an economic condition ... is simplistic, misleading, and false; poverty is a state of mind, a matter of horizons."

Ray Inman—"The beauty of having a low income is that there is not enough money to buy what you don't really need."

Bette Davis—"To fulfill a dream, to be allowed to sweat over lonely labor, to be given a chance to create, is the meat and potatoes of life. The money is the gravy."

Kate Seredy—"I make money using my brains and lose money listening to my heart. But in the long run my books balance pretty well."

Jonathan Swift—"A wise man should have money in his head, but not in his heart."

You may have concluded that I begged the question "Outliving Your Money?" And if you were expecting a financial answer to this question, I can understand your concern. However, I write with the thought that everyone ought to outlive his or her money. Live above and beyond what money can buy and do. When money has done all that it can and must do for us in this life, it can't go beyond this life. As one preacher noted, "I've never seen a hearse with a U-haul trailer behind it."

Mom understands this. This morning I received an email from my sister Marylyn that ices the cake on answering how much money it takes to enjoy a meaningful retirement. She wrote: "I called Mom and had a good visit. How can someone make little blue flowers in a flower bed and tomatoes growing on a vine sound like the Academy Awards? Isn't that wonderful?" Yes, it *is* wonderful.

You and I can go beyond this life and receive the kind of treasure laid up for us in heaven. We can outlive our money both now and forever.

◄ Reflections

- In all your life, recall when you have had the least money and the most money. What difference did the amount of money make in your happiness?

- What are the different ways you've made or gotten money in your life? Which of those ways gave you the most joy and satisfaction?

- Was the money you made in life worth the price you paid for it?

- Reflect on some gifts you have received and some gifts you have given. Which have given you more enjoyment, the receiving or the giving?

- Evaluate your past stewardship of money by answering these questions. Have you invested it? buried it? gained it? lost it? wasted it? saved it? gave it? worshiped it? used it? thought too much of it? thought too little of it? had the right perspective and balance about it?

Projections ►

- How do you plan to use and invest your total assets for the next five years?

- As a result of reading this chapter, identify which of the "Ten Financial Guidelines for Retirement" you need to focus most on. Plan to put into motion one of those guidelines this week. For example, contact an attorney or advisor to update your will.

- If you or your spouse were to die today, would the surviving mate know the total financial picture and what actions to take? It would be a gift of love to make yes the answer to this question.

- Identify your current stewardship attitudes and practices about money and possessions. If you were to project a five-year stewardship plan, what would change in your attitude and practices?
- What are your plans to outlive your money?

Retirement Words from The Word

"Suppose one of you wants to build a tower. Will he not first sit down and estimate the cost to see if he has enough money to complete it?" (Luke 14:28).

"Now listen, you who say, 'Today or tomorrow we will go to this or that city, spend a year there, carry on business and make money.' Why, you do not even known what will happen tomorrow. ...Instead, you ought to say, 'If it is the Lord's will, we will live and do this or that' " (James 4:13–15).

"Well done, thou good and faithful servant: thou hast been faithful over a few things, I will make thee ruler over many things: enter thou into the joy of thy lord" (Matt. 25:21, KJV).

"Bring ye all the tithes into the storehouse" (Mal. 3:10).

"Lay up for yourselves treasure in heaven, where neither moth nor rust doth corrupt, and where thieves do not break through nor steal: For where your treasure is, there will your heart be also" (Matt. 6:20–21, KJV).

"It is more blessed to give than to receive" (Acts 20:35).

"Do not be anxious ...for your heavenly Father knows that you need all these things. But seek first His kingdom and His righteousness; and all these things shall be added to you" (Matt. 6:31–33, NASB).

Prayer

Father, help us to be wise stewards of all we have and to trust You for all we need. Where there is poverty, help us to share from our resources. Help us not to bury our resources in fear or anxiety but to take considered risks and not waste opportunities to increase what You've entrusted to us. Help us to have the right perspective toward money and to use it well. And give us wisdom to outlive our money. *Amen.*

Writing Life's Last Chapter

I am living in life's last chapter, and it is best of all.
—Elton Trueblood

Life is like a book, and it has to come to an end. Elton Trueblood used this comparison when he wrote, "Each chapter of life is good, and it is good to know in which chapter you are living. I'm living in life's last chapter, and it is best of all." He was in his eighties when he stated this conviction, and he died at age ninety-four. The context for his writing was a rich lifetime of productivity that didn't end until he had finished writing life's last chapter—the one titled "Life's Best Chapter: Retirement."

Elton's best and last chapter of life was one relatively long chapter that contained a number of mini-chapters. And when that lengthy chapter of retirement climaxed the book of his earthly life, he likely would have added "amen" to his earlier conviction that the last chapter was best of all. Trueblood wrote more than thirty books, taught and mentored generations of students, traveled worldwide, retired—or semi-retired—and wrote his autobiography. Time and again he told me and I restate it to you, "Don't retire from everything at once. Rather, retire gradually from one thing at a time as you have to and want to." And that's what he did. His writing became newsletters instead of books. He gradually quit traveling to speak and teach but opened his home and heart and mind to those who came to him for mentoring. He did not leave life's last chapter unwritten.

Elton Trueblood was born in 1900, and he considered 1900 to still be part of the nineteenth century. His goal was to live at least until 2001 so he could say that he had lived in three centuries. Although he missed his goal by several years, what he wrote etched the book of his life into eternity. And now he lives beyond time. It is his kind of model that inspires me and also makes me want to encourage others to write all of life's last chapter with excellence—an excellence that deserves the title "Life's Best Chapter: Retirement."

When a friend asked me about my book, I told him I had titled it *Life's Best Chapter: Retirement*. Then he looked into my eyes and asked, "And have you found it to be the best?" I was glad to say yes—so far. And I told him why. And that's what this chapter is about.

Life's Best Chapter?

How can the last chapter of life be the best one, when it ends in death? Realistically, we have to admit that our bodies are wearing out as we groan with arthritis or some other "itis." Most of us struggle in one way or another as we try to see, hear, chew, move around, remember, and stay in charge of our lives. Life's early physical pleasures eventually diminish, and we're challenged in new ways almost every day. So is retirement really life's best chapter? And what about writing the end of that chapter?

I can't honestly say that retirement is the best chapter of life for everyone. This would be inaccurate. Experiencing the best chapter in retirement is not automatic. Writing the retirement chapter of life and making it the best of all chapters calls for wisdom, commitment, perspective, energy, endurance, and undying faith in the Author and Finisher of our faith. With those givens, retirement truly can be life's best chapter all the way to the end. And so far that's my testimony.

Ways the Last Chapter Is Best

Someone wrote, "The pleasures of old age are not less than those of youth, but they are different." I tend to agree with this statement. In some ways the difference between our younger years and older years is like stew. A new batch of stew tastes good, but later bowls of that same stew move from good to delicious as the seasonings take hold. The last chapter of life is well-seasoned, but it also has new ingredients that make it different. With these thoughts in mind, here are some ways that the last chapter of life seems best to me.

The last chapter builds on other chapters and becomes climactic.

Just as we dread coming to the end of a great book we're reading, we're often not ready to finish the book of our lives on earth. But part of reading a book is coming to the end and finishing it. So the last chapter of life is a natural part of the book that provides completion. "Writing Life's Last Chapter" is about everything I've said to you so far and also about bringing the earthly book of life to a climactic end. We don't want the book to end. But it has to. And how the books ends is important.

The last chapter is "Shalom."

As I understand it, this Hebrew greeting is a wish for peace; but it is more than a wish for the absence of conflict.

It is also a wish for God's highest blessings. The last chapter of life can reach a new level of "shalom"—peace and blessings after the storms. Although there are storms of life in retirement, life no longer tends to be like living in Tornado Alley or caught up in the traumas of other repeated events that buffet life during the earlier years.

Someone once said that he didn't mind the rat race but would like to have more of the cheese. Regardless of how much or little cheese we have, the rat race is mostly over for most retirees. The hurry of life is over.

Most of the retirees I know enjoy the relative peace of this last chapter. They tend to take the roads less traveled and leave the interstates to those who always seem to be in a tailgating rush. In retirement, most of us find it easier to let God be our pacesetter and our pacemaker.

The last chapter is filled with optional time.

Actually, all of life is optional time since we choose what we will do with it. But the earlier chapters of life tend to be tied to a sense of *have-to* rather than *want-to* in a lot of what we do. In retirement, there is a special sense of freedom in choosing what to do with our time.

Opportunities pop up everywhere, and they are not just obstacles or problems under another name. Retirees who want to can pursue their curiosities, try something new and different, travel near or far, gain new skills, become a Good Samaritan instead of a passerby priest or Levite, and say yes or no to requests for their time. As my octogenarian mother often says in a girlish tone, "We can just do what we want to." This hasn't been true for most of her life. As the eldest of eight children in a farm family, she was almost a co-mother in their raising. And after a brief respite at marriage, she began to raise her own children until life's last chapter finally offered her more free time.

Even now what she chooses to do is mostly to help others in any way she can.

The last chapter is harvest time for satisfaction.

Wise retirees let regrets sift through the sieve of life, and they prefer to focus on recalling the satisfactions of life's experiences. Despite the problems that occur in each succeeding generation of a family, there is a joy when we retirees see part of our best genes at work in succeeding generations of children, grandchildren, and great-grandchildren. In this satisfaction, we realize that in a sense the last chapter will not be the end of our lives on earth even after we're gone. This benefit of retirement is reserved for those whose thanksgiving for blessings is greater than their griefs over the losses and scars of life.

The last chapter is time to celebrate the present.

The past and future are important seasons of life, but we often let them steal the present moment. As I have listened to people the world over, I have heard them worship a golden past or a utopian future—each of which likely never is a part of reality.

In the changing seasons of each year, I've noticed that comments I make about enjoying the present often draw a contrary response from others. For example, if I comment on the warmth of summer or the fresh air of fall, someone is likely to make it known that they prefer the past season or one yet to come over the present season. It's sad not to enjoy the present seasons of life.

Retirement is both the autumn and sunset of life. It is a time to celebrate without letting anyone steal the present. Although winter and sunset come next, it is a waste to let the autumn go unappreciated or the thought of darkness ruin the sunset. Furthermore, after each winter there is springtime; and after each night, there is a sunrise. The Christian retiree knows that the same will be true after this life. But for now, it's time to celebrate the present.

These are just a few of the many ways that the last chapter can be the best of all chapters. But there are more valuable tips on how to go about writing life's last chapter. So let's take a look at them.

Say Yes to All of Life

Psychologist Paul Tournier was convinced that those who write the earlier chapters of life positively and successfully are most likely to do a great job in writing life's last chapter. His reference point for success isn't a person's title, money, fame, name, health, or other circumstance. Rather, his reference point is whether a person chooses to live each stage of life fully and say *yes* to it.

Tournier saw the successful writing of the last chapter of life as the final *yes* in life. In his book *Learn to Grow Old,* he writes, "A single *yes* goes through the whole of life. It is successively *yes* to childhood, to youth, to adult life, to old age, and finally *Yes!* to death. It is easier to turn over a page of life when we have filled it right up. The Bible talks of the patriarchs who died in peace because they had lived their full span of years (Gen. 25:8)." Tournier wrote both out of experience and conviction when he stated, "My old age has meaning. I can live through it with my gaze still fixed before me, and not behind me, because I am on my way to a destination beyond death."

One bad page or one bad chapter doesn't necessarily make a bad book. Ideally, a book is consistently good from beginning to end. None of us is perfect, so as we write the book of our lives there will be bad chapters and entries. Still, we can fully affirm the facts of each chapter of life with a *yes* as we move on to the next chapter. Those of us who are inclined to say *yes* to life's last chapter—including death—will write it well.

For those who haven't said *yes* to each stage of life, there is still hope as they come to life's last chapter. This hope requires a conversion, a transformation, an about-face that moves from the negative to the positive. The kind of change I'm talking about is not possible for the individual to make alone. Rather, it is the experience of coming to know God in Christ as one's personal Lord and Savior. (See John 3:16-18; Romans 10:9–13; Ephesians 2:8–10.)

When a person quits saying *no* and surrenders with a trusting *yes* to God's gift of grace, it is then that he is born again and is transformed (John 3:1-10; Rom. 12:1–2). It is best to learn to say this *yes* early in life; but if that experience hasn't occurred by retirement, it is essential for the birth of hope in life's last chapter. Now is the time to say *yes* to God and to the rest of life. Then the end of life's book will not be the end of life; rather, the first book will be far surpassed by its sequel in eternal life—which begins with *yes* and never ends.

Live beyond Your Age

What is your RealAge?

A friend of mine introduced me to an Internet site that gives a quick test to estimate biological *RealAge* against chronological age (http://www.RealAge.com). I answered the questions on the test as honestly as I could at my present chronological age of sixty-two. Almost immediately I got back the evaluation that my biological *RealAge* is 59.2 years. Most of us retirees like to hear that we're younger than we are—whether it's an estimation based on scientific data or whether someone just tells us that we look younger than we are. But my RealAge barely brought a smile to my face because I know about the brevity of life, about mortality, and that life is much more than the number of calendar years we live.

Consider your mortality.

As in all of life, people in retirement die at different ages. Unless someone takes his own life, it is anyone's guess when a person will breathe in his last breath and let it out in death. In an average age of 78 years, there are 683,280 hours or 2.4 billion seconds. At 8,760 hours per year, it doesn't take long to estimate how much time you have left. And it seems that most folks don't look at how long they've lived as much as they consider how much life they have left—apart from accident, disease, or violence.

Learn about quality of life.

Although the length of life is uncertain, facing death is certain. None of us can choose how long we will live, but we can choose how we will write today's page and this last chapter we're living in. The quantity of life—figured biologically or by the calendar—is not nearly as important as the quality of life.

Writing life's last chapter well, regardless of how long or short the chapter is, depends on the daily stands we take, the convictions we hold, and the choices we make. The point is this: Don't let the condition of your body or the number of years you live determine your quality of life.

Take Charge of Life's Last Chapter

Choose life.

Some retirees choose to withdraw from active life and live with shriveled up spirits long before physical death occurs. They choose a kind of living death before the funeral instead of choosing life in the face of death. I agree with Jack London: "The proper function of man is to live, not to exist. I shall not waste my days trying to prolong them. ...I shall use my time." The Bible itself says, "I have set before you life and death ... therefore choose life" (Deut. 30:19). In retirement we can choose to write the last chapter with life rather than death—as climax rather than anticlimax. The choice is ours.

Seize life's opportunities.

The condition of a person's inner spirit is above and beyond biology and chronology in determining the value of a person's life. To say it another way, great-souled people stay young despite aging bodies; and they live decisive, positive lives. In the Greek language there are two words for time: *chronos* and *kairos*. *Chronos* is any old time—just a chronicle or chronology of life. But *kairos* means opportune time. The person whose inner spirit stays young and alive keeps on making timely decisions that result in life's super moments. And it is never too late.

Don't let dying stop your living.

Sociology professor Morrie Schwarz had seemingly said *yes* to all the chapters in life when he was diagnosed with Lou Gehrig's disease (amyotrophic lateral sclerosis, or ALS). This diagnosis was a death sentence—this disease would slowly and agonizingly waste Morrie's body from legs to lungs until it would kill him. He would begin to lose the use of his body but not his mind.

Morrie had been the professor, mentor, and friend to Mitch Albom, who became an award-winning sports writer. Twenty years after Mitch's college experience and a while after Morrie had contracted ALS, Mitch came back to

Morrie for one final, informal "course" on living and dying. His book *Tuesdays with Morrie* grew out of that course.

In effect Morrie was writing life's last chapter, and he knew the chapter would be a short one. Besides all the other feelings and emotions Morrie had, he decided early on whether to withdraw and die or to live life as fully as possible in the time he had left. He chose life. He chose to live as long as possible with dignity, courage, humor, composure, and love. He refused to be ashamed of dying, and he refused to equate dying with uselessness. He did not see dying as a reason to quit living.

With a lack of self-pity and a refusal to surrender to depression, Morrie began what might be considered his best chapter of life as a professor. As he said, everyone knows they're going to die but no one believes it. He shared what he himself had experienced: namely, that when you have come face-to-face with death and learn not to fear it, then you're free to live.

Morrie became a catalyst to teach and challenge people to separate the wheat from the chaff in life and to learn how to bring meaning into their lives. He taught that the last chapter is not too late to get involved in life. The way Morrie wrote that last chapter of his life challenges all of us as we write our own last chapter. And that chapter can be magnificent.

Decide how busy you will be.

Perhaps there ought to be an eleventh commandment for retirees: namely, "Don't whine that you're too busy." Retirees have more optional time than ever, but the quantity of our leisure time often seems to make it harder to organize and manage productively than ever before.

The fact that our remaining time in this life is limited is no reason to crowd it with activities that seemingly have no priority. We live life's last chapter best when we choose to pace ourselves. Good time management isn't a crushing schedule that causes emotional claustrophobia. Rather, it is the deliberate choice to live life decently and in order by giving priority to what is most meaningful in life. It's true that some chapters of life are busier and more hectic than others, but it is equally true that our personal choices affect our own attitude about how busy we will be. This fact especially applies to retirement.

Again and again I am reminded of the brevity of Jesus' life and His awareness of how brief His time on earth would be. At about age thirty Jesus fully knew He was living life's last earthly chapter. Yet He never seemed to rush and never counted Himself too busy to help others. He who was dying said, "I am the way, the truth, and the life" (John 14:6). In obedience to His Father, He said *yes* to every chapter of life and chose to write the last chapter with life—for Himself and for all of us. Jesus lived life productively, positively, decisively, and according to God's timing.

Get Your Affairs in Order

When I was a Boy Scout, I learned a valuable lesson for all of life: "Be prepared!" This motto is especially important for life's last chapter.

Check your spiritual life.

I've shared in an earlier chapter the experience I once had on a jetliner. The pilot came on the intercom and told us we would need to prepare for a crash landing because of a possible malfunction in the landing gear. As we circled the airport to use up fuel, I began to check my spiritual life. I was ready to live or die because I had already accepted Christ as Lord and Savior. Fortunately the landing gear held and we landed safely. But my peace and ultimate safety did not depend on a landing gear. These depended on my relationship to God in Christ. This preparation has priority over all other affairs that need to be in order.

When Henry David Thoreau was dying, a priest asked him if he had made his peace with God. Thoreau answered, "I was not aware that we had quarreled." Everyone has quarreled with God, and we all need to make peace with Him (Rom. 3:23; 6:23; 10:9–10).

Check your human relationships.

Is everything all right between you and the rest of your family? Do you need to ask or give forgiveness? Are your friendships in good repair? Is there anything you want to say to someone or do for that person before life's last chapter closes? Now is the time to speak and act. Then there won't be any regrets. When my dad died, I spoke at his funeral. I was glad to say that our family didn't have any regrets. We had pretty well said or done all that we needed to while life was still here. Dad left a heritage, a legacy, quotations, and memories. And though he has gone to be with the Lord, in a sense he's still with us because of what he left us.

Check your financial matters.

Is your will up-to-date? Are your bills paid or provided for in your estate? Does your spouse know what the widowed survivor's financial condition will be? Have you chosen an executor for your estate, and are you satisfied with that choice? If you were left behind to settle your own estate, are things the way you would like for them to be? You may want to update some things, share some financial information with family members or others, collect financial records and put them together in one place. And if all this seems like too much trouble, you might just want to enlist someone to do the detail work to your satisfaction.

Make your wishes known.

Besides having a formal will, there's a certain satisfaction in passing on possessions to the ones you would like to have them. There may be diaries or journals that you want to make available to all family members, to be preserved as part of the family heritage and history. I've kept a diary most of my life. One of my reasons for this discipline has been to share my life experiences with my descendants as they write the book of their lives.

In living life's last chapter, there ought not be anything morbid or foreboding about sharing what you would like to happen after you die. Morris Schwarz decided to have a living funeral for himself. He invited who he wanted to be there and planned what would take place. So, while he was still alive he conducted his own funeral. But most of us leave our funeral to others. They would probably appreciate knowing our wishes, and they would likely find comfort and joy in trying to carry out those wishes. (That is, if these are reasonable wishes.) This might include who will perform the funeral, your favorite songs, and Scriptures you'd like to have read. Your place of burial might already be decided or need to be decided. Cremation has become more popular in recent years; and although this is a matter of personal choice, it sometimes needs some sensitive sharing with other family members. And there may be other affairs you need or want to get in order. In life's last chapter, there is a special joy in being prepared.

Exchange Your Tent for a Mansion

We all have an earthly body that grows older and eventually wears out. In 2 Corinthians 4:16–5:10, Paul compares our body to a tent. In those days, tents were usually made of skin. Paul was confident that the earthly tent of Christian believers would be exchanged for a house not made with hands, one fit for all eternity (2 Cor. 5:1). Jesus spoke of this house as a mansion (John 14:2, KJV). Contemporary translators use the term "dwelling place" or "room." But I like what many preachers have said: "Can you imagine a house in heaven being less than a mansion?" So I prefer to think of exchanging a tent for a mansion.

Once in a Bible study I was teaching on this subject, I asked a young woman named Judy to share with the class about her Canadian honeymoon that involved camping out in a leaky tent. She shared in detail the discomfort of living in a tent. Then I added my punch line: "You see, a tent gets old, wears out, and is not as good as a house." Unprompted, Judy added, "And the tent never was as good as a house."

I learned a great lesson from my pupil: No matter how great or good my earthly body is at any stage of life on earth, it will never be as good as the resurrection body God has in store for me. What stage of your earthly life would you like your resurrection body to be like? Certainly not as it is in the last chapter. But also, not as it has been in any earlier chapter of life. Without our losing recognition or personality, God plans to replace our destroyed tent with a mansion fit for all eternity and better than we've ever known.

So we don't need to worry about what our body has lost and the destruction that has come. We don't need to worry about bodies destroyed in accidents or burned up in fires. God will replace our earthly tents with his heavenly mansions.

Life is a book, and retirement is—or can be—it's best chapter. The last chapter may be short or long but likely it will be made up of a number of mini-chapters. No matter what we decide to do with retirement, we are still responsible to God for being good stewards of His calling. The Bible calls us to "Lead a life worthy of the calling to which you have been called" (Eph. 4:1, NRSV). Writing the last chapter of life continues to be a stewardship that we are entrusted with by the Author and the Finisher of our faith (Heb. 12:2, KJV).

As I finish writing this book and you finish reading it, I pray that the effort we've both made will make life's last chapter grander and will also get us ready for the sequel—to be written in heaven.

In the last analysis, God will judge for each of us whether retirement was life's best chapter. If we choose God as our Coauthor and write it according to His will, there's a good chance retirement will be life's best chapter.

◄ *Reflections*

- Look back at the Table of Contents and spend a moment reflecting on the chapter titles and what you remember from the chapters you've read.

- To conserve what you've read, look through the book to see what you've underlined, penciled in the margin, or made notes on; and add any notes you might want to come back to.

- Identify something in this book that has already made a difference in your retirement life.

- Think through the last chapter of this book and reflect on how you're writing life's last chapter in the book of your life.

Projections ►

- I've written this book with the hope that it will make a difference in the lives of those who read it. With this in mind, join with me in some assumptions that could make a difference in your life.

- Assume that life's last chapter for you will contain at least five mini-chapters of one year each. Identify one priority, project, or activity you would like to write with your life in each of those years.

- What if life's last chapter for you should end one year from now? Considering that possibility, make a checklist from this chapter and from your own mind and heart of what you would want to get in order to complete the book of your life. Commit to do at least one of those items on your checklist this week.

- If you were asked to *rewrite* this book on retirement,

what would you add to the book to make retirement life's best chapter? List at least one or two items. Then make sure your life matches what you have added or plan steps to make these items part of your last chapter.

- Suppose an editor asked you to write a book on retirement that majors on hope, joy, productivity, and positive living. And suppose the book must come from your own retirement experiences. Could you do it? If not, what would have to change for you to be able to write such a book?

- Now, from one author to another, here's my final suggestion: Get a journal and start writing your life's last chapter. Determine to make it life's best chapter. Happy writing!

Retirement Words from The Word

"In your hearts set apart Christ as Lord. Always be prepared to give an answer to everyone who asks you to give the reason for the hope that you have" (1 Peter 3:15).

"Abraham breathed his last and died at a good old age, an old man and full of years; and he was gathered to his people" (Gen. 25:8).

"Choose life, so that you and your children may live and that you may love the LORD your God, listen to his voice, and hold fast to him. For the LORD is your life" (Deut. 30:19–20).

"Be very careful, then, how you live—not as unwise but as wise, making the most of every opportunity, because the days are evil" (Eph. 5:15).

"You yourselves are our letter, written on our hearts, known and read by everybody. You show that you are a letter from Christ, the result of our ministry, written not with ink but with the Spirit of the living God" (2 Cor. 3:2–3).

"Now we know that if the earthly tent we live in is destroyed, we have a building from God, an eternal house in heaven, not built by human hands" (2 Cor. 5:1).

"I think it is right to refresh your memory as long as I live in the tent of this body, because I know that I will soon put it aside, as our Lord Jesus Christ has made clear to me. And I will make every effort to see that after my departure you will always be able to remember these things" (2 Peter 1:13–15).

"For as in Adam all die, even so in Christ shall all be made alive. ...The last enemy that shall be destroyed is death" (1 Cor. 15:22,26).

"I am now ready to be offered, and the time of my departure is at hand. I have fought a good fight, I have finished my course, I have kept the faith: Henceforth there is laid up for me a crown of righteousness, which the Lord, the righteous judge, shall give me at that day" (2 Tim. 4:6–8).

Prayer

Father, help us to enjoy the blessings of retirement and be aware of our stewardship responsibility to live it productively all the way to the end of this earthly life. May we have wisdom not to retire from everything at once, motivation to continue choosing life, and courage to face dying without giving up living. And may we trust You to help us complete this book of life and Your promise to exchange our tents for mansions.

Amen.